STALINGRAD

The Decisive Battle of the Eastern Front

STALINGRAD

The Decisive Battle of the Eastern Front

By

John Mansfield

Vij Books

New Delhi (India)

Published by

Vij Books
(*An Imprint of Vij Books India Pvt Ltd*)
(Publishers, Distributors & Importers)
4836/24, 3rd Floor, Ansari Road
Delhi – 110 002
Phone: 91-11-43596460
Mobile: 98110 94883
e-mail: contact@vijpublishing.com
www.vijbooks.in

ISBN: 978-81-19438-92-1 (PB)

Contents

Chapter 1

Prelude to Disaster: Operation Barbarossa

The Genesis of Operation Barbarossa: Ideology, Strategy, and Miscalculations

Operation Barbarossa was rooted in Adolf Hitler's strong belief in Lebensraum – 'living space' and his aim to remove communism from Europe. The German dictator wanted to expand his empire eastwards into the Soviet Union so that there would be enough land and resources for the German people. For Hitler, this was driven by his intense hatred for communism, which he saw as a direct threat to achieving his dream of establishing a racially purified and powerful state. All these ideas converged and led to what became one of the largest military undertakings in human history.

The actual planning for this attack started in the summer of 1940 when the Wehrmacht High Command worked out a detailed plan to defeat Russia quickly. The main people involved in developing this strategy were Generaloberst Franz Halder, who was chief of staff of the Army General Staff and had overall responsibility for drawing up operational plans; Hermann Göring – head Luftwaffe (German Air Force) – ensured that his service would have complete control over the skies necessary support ground troops during the offensive operations. Other key participants included Adolf Hitler himself providing general direction as well an ideological basis for what he wanted to be achieved from such a campaign; Hermann Göring, who made sure air superiority could be gained over the entire front, thus enabling success at lower levels but above all it had to be total while limited just enough not expend combat power needlessly* – decided that air fleets allotted different areas would strike simultaneously instead rotationally as had been originally envisioned thus allowing production reserves accumulate where they were originally located before being moved forward again thereby increasing numbers available for subsequent attacks

Operation Barbarossa's planning commenced in full swing during the German High Command's detailed strategic formulation of how to bring about a quick and conclusive defeat against the USSR. The key persons taking part in crafting this provision, Chief of General Staff Generaloberst Franz Halder, was responsible for the entire conceptualization while Adolf Hitler gave overall direction ideological underpinning air chief marshal Generaloberst Hermann Göring made sure that his service will possess the sky during the entire operation time. He did so by assigning different theatres to various air fleets which attacked them all at once instead of one after another thus enabling success at lower levels but above all it had to be total while limited just enough not expend combat power needlessly* – decided that air fleets allotted different areas would strike simultaneously instead rotationally as had been originally envisioned thus allowing production reserves accumulate where they were originally located before being moved forward again thereby increasing numbers available for subsequent attacks

The planners had failed to calculate how strong and resourceful the Soviets were. German intelligence was clouded by political prejudices and an absence of accurate information into thinking that the Soviet military was ineffectively armed, poorly led and lacking in spirit. The idea had gained ground in Germany because the Soviet Union had done badly in the Winter War against Finland from 1939 until 1940. Here, the High Command of the German Army wrongly saw nothing but a sign of weakness throughout the system. Therefore they thought if they attacked hard enough so as not allow any time for recovery it would be possible for them to break down Soviet resistance completely within few months and to acquire most important strategic points before winter.

In a departure from previous campaigns which had been based largely upon Blitzkrieg (lightning warfare) techniques involving speed and surprise, those at the top German military leadership realized that their new undertaking would necessitate considerable adjustments owing to Russia's vast size along with its difficult nature. They were nevertheless certain about their capacity to win fast using this kind of strategy anywhere. The plan envisaged an invasion spearheaded by three army groups known as North, Centre and South respectively. The Northern Group commanded by Field Marshal Wilhelm Ritter von Leeb was required to move forward through Baltic States towards Leningrad; The Center Group under Field Marshal Fedor von Bock had as its objective Moscow which was not only capital but also political center of the Soviets ; and finally, The Southern group led by Field-Marshal Gerd von Rundstedt aimed at taking Ukraine and then pushing on southwards towards oil-rich Caucasus.

There were many objectives that drove the strategy of Operation Barbarossa. Fast seizure of Soviet lands - like oil, grain and other raw materials needed to support the war effort and the German economy itself – topped the list. German command saw it necessary to destroy the Red Army as a condition for holding these lands so that there would be no revival on the part of USSR. Leningrad, Moscow or Stalingrad were among important cities that had to be taken. Their fall was significant from a point of strategy but also had great moral value; they were expected to break down the soviet spirit and administrative machine to quicken the state's collapse.

Operation Barbarossa was an ambitious plan with a rather tight schedule. The Germans thought that they would be able to finish off their enemy within few months before severe Russian winter set in thus paralyzing all military activities. This belief originated from an overestimation of oneself caused by successful military operations in Europe; also there was insufficient understanding about volume and difficulty degree at the current stage. Experience gained during lightning campaigns in Poland, France and Balkans made Wehrmacht command believe in its invincibility, perceiving the Soviet Union as another easy walkover.

Operation Barbarossa, in its origin and implementation, was a huge bet which echoed wider strategic and ideological needs of the Nazi regime. It combined determination, and self-confidence which were the main features in Hitlers warfare and reflected his impatience and imprudence in the war. The failure of it demonstrated how dangerous it is when one underrates an enemy's power of resistance and recovery. The beginning and the end of this operation still remain to be a vivid lesson in the history of military strategy and tactics.

Blitzkrieg's Surge: The Initial Onslaught of Operation Barbarossa

Operation Barbarossa, the grandest military invasion in the history of man starting on June 22, 1941 as Nazi Germany sought to crush its former ally through the deployment of millions of troops into Russia. The Soviet Union's swift and powerful onslaught came as little surprise during those initial stages since it employed much of what had worked when conquering Western Europe; however, this time there were three million Axis soldiers backed up by 3000 tanks, 7000 artillery guns and 2500 planes all moving at once - numbers that had never been seen before.

Tank after tank poured over fields or crashed through villages as they headed towards their targets while planes rained bombs down on roads filled with retreating Soviet soldiers who were desperately trying to slow down the enemy's advance. Once successful, these gaps would allow for the encirclement and subsequent annihilation of entire army groups caught within them thus making it impossible for them to extricate themselves.

Furthermore, an offensive of this magnitude demanded constant maintenance; therefore, if left unchecked, sieges could drag on indefinitely. Victories such as these came at grim costs: thousands died every day during battles where both sides fought tooth and nail over every inch gained or lost; millions more perished from starvation, exposure or disease while trapped behind enemy lines without hope of rescue.

Contrastingly, Minsk fell on 28th of June after being encircled just four days earlier on 24th. Another week later, Bialystok met the same fate and by July 16th Smolensk—a city that had taken six bloody weeks to capture during WWI—was also surrounded but this time for less than half as long before surrendering unconditionally on July 27th thereby signaling a major shift in momentum which would soon culminate with Soviet forces breaking through German lines near Moscow.

One of the early victories in the attack was that the German military caught and destroyed Soviet forces during a number of big battles. The Battle of Białystok–Minsk (22 June – 3 July 1941) perfectly demonstrated what they could do. The Wehrmacht's Panzer divisions quickly broke through Russian positions, encircling whole Soviet armies with a lighting speed. When it was all over, there were about 300 thousand prisoners taken by Germans, besides huge amounts of weapons and supplies. This win not only illustrated how good German strategy could be but also left–hand bank Western Bug River region weakened with already weak defences of this part of the USSR against advances towards Moscow by Nazi Germany.

By capturing Minsk on June 28th, 1941, it became possible for them to move deeper into Russia, up to Smolensk, and beyond. The Battle of Smolensk took place from July 10th to September 10th in 1941 which continued this swift advance. It was strategically important for the Germans to take Smolensk because this city stood on the way to Moscow. During the fighting there, they tried to encircle Red Army units defending it but couldn't succeed due strong resistance shown by soviet soldiers who fought till last man. However, several Russian armies were wiped out when German troops surrounded them, inflicting more than 300 thousand casualties among captured soldiers only.

Aftermath of Smolensk had serious consequences for the overall situation during war period at all theatres of operations. It put out of order Soviet control system, compelling high command of Russia (USSR) at that time – STAVKA– to think over again its past mistakes and make new decisions about how best they could protect themselves against future Nazi offensives on wider scales across whole front line with maximum depth possible within available limits while directing main efforts towards main directions along priority axes determined by political leadership taking into account strategic reserve locations required for timely assistance. Meanwhile it raised spirits among Hitlerites who started believing in success but overestimated their strength regarding duration.

Most Important Thing Is That Victory Also Elevates Our Confidence In Winning This Thing Altogether Fast Enough And For Sure Enough. Nevertheless, We Have Come To Realize That We Are Incapable Of Sustaining Such Speed Indefinitely Without Putti... However, it crystally demonstrated at the same time the growing logistical difficulties which arose due to overstretched german supply lines caused mainly because of too rapid advancement causing delays followed by shortages stemming from prolonged maintenance often required after initial stages following enemy contact as well as a lack thereof altogether occasionally occurred whenever expected distributions failed to meet their destinations on schedule causing interruptions.

Operation Barbarossa's initial achievements were attributed to the Panzer divisions, which were essential units in the armours. These were the German combat forces since they had tanks like the Panzer III and IV. They were highly mobile and had much firepower compared to any other military section. With this kind of ability, they could hit deep into the Russian territory while still managing to encircle enemy troops by going around them' thus outflanking them as well. Additionally, combined arms teams created by motorised infantry alongside artillery units operated along Panzer divisions thus making it possible for them to exploit breakthroughs to continue their advance without losing momentum.

Moreover, the Luftwaffe also played a critical role during this period of time when ground offensive support was needed most from above. Once they achieved air supremacy at an early stage into their offensive plan, German planes never stopped bombarding Soviet positions day after day until their supply depots or communication lines got destroyed through constant raids. Not only did such bombings bring about massive deaths among enemy soldiers who could not run away due to being surrounded all over again but also made it hard for them to counterattack since most of their command posts had been hit too bad for anyone inside come out alive. Besides, Stuka dive-bombers offered close air support which was quite effective especially where strong points had been set up by the enemies hence allowing our tanks move fast towards new targets while clearing off any remaining resistance easily along the way.

However, despite these early victories, there were still numerous challenges faced by Germans while advancing further eastwards into Russia. The vast size of this country together with determination shown by its people during defence operations began taking tolls on german forces thus slowing down their speed greatly over time. On top of that pine forests, rivers full of water and dash; and needs bridging materials- as well as marshlands which can rotary wings into something deadly when least expected areas among many others acted accordingly too not forgetting scorched earth policy adopted now then again or something alike (infastructure destruction).

The early stages of Operation Barbarossa showcased the effectiveness of Blitzkrieg tactics and the skill of the German military. In the first few weeks of the invasion, there were rapid advancements and definitive wins that made the success of the operation seem certain. However, difficulties began to arise as early as this because of logistics, increased Soviet resistance, and the sheer size of the land to be captured. What might have appeared as a magnificent start turned out to be just a beginning filled with long struggle sapping away at German military might, during which it bore witness to most extreme limits being put in place shaping events of World War II.

Barbarossa's Achilles Heel: Logistical Challenges and Operational Delays

Operation Barbarossa was the codename for the German invasion of the Soviet Union during World War II. Implemented in 1941, it was a large-scale offensive which aimed for quick victory through the use of Blitzkrieg tactics. However, Wehrmacht's logistical issues slowed them down significantly and were, ultimately, the main reason for the failure of the operation. The Soviet Union was a huge country with terrible roads and extreme weather conditions that made everything several times as hard as it should have been.

Keeping up supply lines across the immense Soviet territories emerged as one of the most challenging logistical problems faced by Wehrmacht. The farther German troops penetrated Russia, the longer distances they had to cover back to their bases in Germany for supplies. Our forces' quick westward movement had been supported by an efficient system of railways within Western Europe but this same network could not handle such rapid eastward advance. Since majority if not all types goods were carried along these lines, their narrow gauge compared to European standards meant that a lot time had to be wasted changing wagons or using slower means which were also less effective.

In addition to this, shortage of capacity was also caused by challenges posed due to inadequate Soviet infrastructure facilities which made things even worse. Roads were mostly made of dirt unsuitable for heavy military traffic because they could not withstand frequent use neither could they be repaired in time before deteriorating further. However, most bridges connecting different parts of the country had been destroyed either intentionally by retreating Red Army units or as collateral damage during air raids carried out my Luftwaffe planes against transportation hubs located near them. Therefore, affected areas where such vital installations were situated had no alternative but wait until new ones were build instead thus leading into congestion points along various sectors comprising overall front line thereby hampering overall logistic support operations aimed at sustaining offensive momentum needed for the successful completion our part of breakthrough phase within overall campaign plan designed by strategic headquarters supreme high command armed forces OKW at that particular juncture Estonian border Belarusian SSR.

As the front lines were pushed farther eastward, keeping the troops supplied with fuel, ammunition and food became more and more problematic. Large amounts of fuel were consumed in the rapid advance that required it to be brought over great distances. The necessity for petrol increased even further because of motorized units and machines of all types. This made the problem of supplying them become a matter of life or death. At the same time, there was never enough ammunition supply since the logistic networks could not keep up with their fast expenditure rates during offensives that lasted for months on end. Moreover, the Germans suffered from hunger frequently due to insufficient rations which led in turn into malnutrition among soldiers affecting negatively their combat capability. It also became clear that relying solely on looting as an alternative way of getting food could not work indefinitely without causing additional tensions between occupiers and locals.

The Russian climate and geography posed further problems which often proved beyond solution. The intense heat and dust of a Russian summer exacted its toll both on men and machines. The autumn rains commonly referred to as 'Rasputitsa' turned roads into quagmires thus limiting movement severely and complicating supply. Vehicles got stuck in mud while supplies could hardly move because they had to be pulled manually along such roads. It was difficult enough supplying armies so far away but when one considers the nature of country - forest land, swampy regions intersected by numerous rivers etcetera - which lay between them, this task assumed gigantic proportions. All these natural obstacles required elaborate engineering works; consequently still more labour had to be diverted from fighting at the front.

Winter brought a new set of difficulties altogether, ones for which German military forces weren't prepared whatsoever. Even their substantial training exercises in Norway had left them ill-equipped to cope with this climate when it arrived on Russian soil. The bitter cold , often thirty degrees below zero Centigrade or even lower , caused equipment break-downs , frost-bite among personnel and great loss of life through exposure . Lack dress suited for such weather proved fatal many times over especially since troops were frequently obliged live under canvas during periods when temperatures never rose above freezing point day after day . The cold also interfered greatly with automotive transport which fact coupled together with arms becoming sluggish made whole Wehrmacht almost useless as a weapon battle thus having catastrophic effect upon her fortunes throughout rest of the campaign.

Logistically, it wasn't just operational delays; the Soviets also played a significant part through resistance and counterattacks. The Red Army suffered massive initial losses when it was caught off guard but eventually pulled itself together and fought back fiercely. These attacks on the part of the Soviets usually came at very crucial times as they interfered with German supply lines which made it necessary for them to redirect some of their troops into defensive positions so as not to be cut off entirely. Consequently, this caused German advancement be halted giving them time to reorganize at will thus stabilizing the front line hence making it difficult for any further progress to be made by their enemies.

Another key decision that had a major impact on delaying operations involved diverting forces for capturing Kiev instead of going straight for Moscow. This move was aimed at securing strategic objectives in the south while also cutting off important resources from falling into enemy hands however; these actions served only to slow down any advancement towards the Soviet capital city. Although successful tactically since over 600,000 Red Army soldiers were surrounded there but strategically too costly due to time taken by defenders around Moscow who fortified their positions awaiting attack which never came until much later when everything had changed already anyway.

These delays were further worsened by internal disputes and shifts in strategic direction among the top echelons of German command. Insisting that certain economic targets like oil fields located within Caucasus region should also be taken captur

Wehrmacht faced several challenges during Operation Barbarossa due to logistics and operational delays which shows that it's difficult to carry out large scale military operations over a wide area where the climate is bad. At first this attack succeeded because German troops moved so fast using Blitzkrieg tactics but later they could not get enough supplies for fighting against USSR and Russian soldiers did not give up easily too. So all these problems together made sure that instead of shortening the time required for achieving victory over Soviet Union as much as possible, there would be a very long bloody war with significant material costs for all parties involved.

The Soviet Counterstrike: Defence and Adaptation Against Barbarossa

At the start of Operation Barbarossa in June 1941, the Germans caught the Soviets with their pants down. The Red Army was shocked, but it was also quick to mobilize. This helped them save a bit of face, among other things.

Initially, Stalin was not very helpful. When he heard about it all, he did not believe that the Germans had done anything. He thought it was a trick. Consequently, this made things worse for everyone involved because there would have been more time if this had not happened—and time is often very important when wars are concerned—but then again maybe not? I'm not sure.

However, the Soviet leadership were eventually able to respond effectively. Intelligence had been pointing towards an impending invasion for some time now; we should have seen it coming really. The borders were heavily fortified but this did not deter them in the slightest bit so I guess you could say our defenses were a little bit ineffective…

The unexpected assault led to immediate losses of territory. The invaders were simply too fast for us. They moved quicker than we thought humanly possible which is kind of scary if you stop and think about it too hard because like what if they were superhuman robots or something? Weird…

In addition, the command structure was not designed for flexibility. It was very rigid. Every decision had to go all the way up through channels that didn't allow for much bending or twisting along 'em so by time anything could be done about anything everything had pretty much already happened which isn't great when you think about how preventable most things always seem in retrospect but hey ho such as life goes on at least until end comes knocking at door etc etc.

The first step taken by the Soviet Union after being invaded, was for them to be in complete disarray. This meant that they didn't know what was going on or what they should do about it. There were literally no plans for anything at all except sitting around eating ice cream and hoping everything would somehow work itself out, which obviously isn't very realistic, but then again, neither are most things when you really stop thinking too much.

The Red Army's ability to deploy its reserves quickly was facilitated by the strategic importance of the Soviet rail network, which allowed for the movement of troops and supplies over large distances at high speed. In addition, it became clear that this rail network made it possible for the Soviets fill in gaps in their defences without delay and create more solid defensive lines. The depth and scale of Soviet manpower aided by railway usage enabled them hold out in prolonged defensive operations notwithstanding heavy initial losses.

During the course of the invasion, Soviet forces started changing their tactics so as not be defeated through German blitzkrieg. They introduced deep battle strategy characterized by counterattacks within taken positions and defense in width more closer home. The primary purpose was absorbing shock but eventually attriting away at an enemy roomed in by fortifications while responding with offensive measures where necessary up until a breakthrough for encirclement could be achieved or breakthrough attained in other parts while leaving some reserves behind.

Soviet defensive walls provided covers behind which counteroffensives were prepared while time was bought waiting for reserves mobilization. These included networks upon networks bunkers designed specifically obstructing armoured columns infantry attacks German forward movements posed on them. meanwhile delaying points such as Moscow city since Leningrad where German resources had been tied up in besieging it rather than advancing further westward, were also created during world war two against nazi germany.

To keep the readability high and also elaborating the defence of Moscow, additional counteroffensives were mounted which caused significant losses for the Germans and disrupted their plans, like those at Smolensk and Kiev.

Behind enemy lines, acts of sabotage were carried out by these groups ambushing supply convoys, destroying infrastructure and collecting information among other things thus greatly interfering with the German supply lines and communication system making it more difficult for the Wehrmacht logistically.

In addition to this, despite suffering initial reverses, swift Soviet counterattacks soon blunted the edge of German offensive thrusts. The early counteroffensives bore witness to Red Army's resilience and ability to resist organizedly although they proved expensive and only partly successful in most cases. Such as the operations around Moscow itself that began from October 1941 until December when there was a turning point during World War Two.

The Battle of Moscow started in October 1941 and ended with the Soviet Union's counteroffensive in December of that year; it marked a change in the tides for them. As German troops closed on towards their capital city, Moscow, winter set in coupled with increased Soviet resistance which finally brought Wehrmacht to halt within city limits too. The counteroffensive started on December 5 exploited both severe weather conditions created by this time and also overextended lines typical during such periods as well thereby pushing back those who had besieged her gate, thus giving birth to what became known famously later on–The great turning point battles fought against Nazi Germany sited mainly towards eastern part of Europe continent besides other regions involved during second world war.

Coordination between different Soviet fronts was essential for the success of these counteroffensives. The Stavka played a crucial role in directing operations across the vast Eastern Front, ensuring that different fronts could support each other and concentrate forces at critical points. Soviet leadership, including figures such as Generals Zhukov and Timoshenko, demonstrated adaptability and strategic acumen in orchestrating these complex operations. The ability to coordinate large-scale movements and attacks across multiple fronts was a testament to the organisational capacity of the Soviet military and its command structure.

The Soviet response to Operation Barbarossa was a multifaceted and dynamic process that evolved rapidly in the face of existential threat. From the initial shock and disorganisation, the Soviet Union harnessed its vast resources, strategic depth, and capacity for rapid adaptation to mount a formidable defence and eventually go on the offensive. The combination of early defensive measures, tactical innovations, and coordinated counteroffensives ultimately blunted the German advance and set the stage for the protracted and gruelling conflict that would define the Eastern Front in the years to come.

The Road To Stalingrad: Strategy, Preparation, And Initial Movements

In the German campaign on the Eastern Front, Stalingrad was a vital goal for them and there were several strategic requirements, careful planning and intense initial clashes in the approach to that city. There were a number of reasons why the decision was made to make Stalingrad the target for attack by German forces over and above its purely industrial value.

The importance of Stalingrad strategically was many-sided. It bore the name of Joseph Stalin, head of the USSR, and therefore had tremendous symbolic significance as an embodiment of the morale and industrial potentialities of that country. The fall of Stalingrad would be a great psychological blow to Russia; this was also understood in German propaganda which sought constantly to underrate her fighting qualities and staying power in the war. From the industrial point of view too it was important because there lay a knot of factories producing tanks, guns and other munitions necessary for carrying on the struggle against Germany – which though unrecognized by many people is still our foe!

Further, the City acted as a hub in transportation system due to its position on western bank of Volga river where goods could be shifted from one part of USSR to another; hence logistically it became significant also geographically since would sever this route between Northern and Southern Russia; therefore making shipping impossible up or down stream along any portion thereof without first taking such control away from her defenders as they might establish behind themselves.

Among other things too there were certain advantages offered by nature herself but not unattended with difficulties either—such being merely matters outside common knowledge among those who have never studied military science seriously enough perhaps before now … However situated upon said River gave them such an advantage because they could use it both for defense against any attack as well as means attack; and at same time control over traffic upon said river … It was also appreciated that within built up area with many industrial works within it would be very hard indeed to dislodge them from positions once established thereabouts--for this reason areas like these were called 'fortresses'. Nevertheless if we took possession ourselves then matter would be different altogether!

But from our point view how should we regard Stalingrad? According to their plan if they could capture city this act alone might well have ensured success in general terms too – at least that is what our enemies believed about us … For if we lost such place which had been fortified by nature herself none other could take its without almost certain heaviest losses possible under any circumstances whatever … This was recognised even by those who were ignorant most things concerning war history altogether up till then because it had always been so said frequently always found true afterwards according reliable authority wherever any statement might be made relating to military matters no matter where such assertion may originally come from neither should anyone allow themselves assume otherwise whatever … Because unfortunately although many people wish make out differently there are some truths which cannot altered while others however desirable quite simply do not exist for instance there is nothing whatever gained whatever through pretending otherwise when reality tells us quite otherwise already along these lines etcetera etcetera etc.

The German High Command noticed after the first stages of Operation Barbarossa that they needed to gather together again before they could carry on an attack towards the south for a long time. The first attack used up a lot of their power and made them see where they had weak points in their plans. In order to do this, they started again from the beginning. These weak points were mainly in logistics. It was decided, as a result of these considerations, there would be concentration on Stalingrad which was expected to lead to a quick win that would paralyze the whole Soviet war potential thereby opening way into Caucasus. The effort was to be made not so much by the attack itself as by its effect upon overall situation.

To get ready for fighting in Stalingrad area it was decided to concentrate large double underlined amounts of men and materials at this point. This was done by the Germans placing Army Group South under Field Marshal von Bock initially but later General Paulus. The redeployment saw Panzer divisions ,infantry units and air fleets moved from elsewhere to the southern front. There was also extensive use made of air power in this operation carried out with aim similar soften defences before ground troops advanced thus saving many lives also known as propaganda approach that Americans use these days against Iraq instead killing civilians directly but a little slower nonetheless but still in large quantities always attached collateral damage reports monthly basis cumulatively adding up annually doesn't really matter if you think about math but yeah just trust me alright; nobody ever really reads them).

Intelligence was another crucial aspect during preparations for battle at Stalingrad. There were extensive attempts made by

Abwehr a German military organization responsible for counter-intelligence internally within theWehrmacht and Luftwaffe Air Force unit conducting recon on Soviet defensive systems around Stalingrad area trying to figure out where they were weakest or strongest they being those same defences referred just now . In this case that meant trying to find gaps between different positions such as trenches bunkers minefields etcetera etcetera more from all over town stuff like those hills up north east west south it doesn't really matter what direction specifically because there are so many hills around here might even say some would argue there's nothing else besides them hills plus this river but then again who knows maybe somebody else thinks differently although probably not likely given current situation concerning said hills near aforementioned river anyway moving right along now aren't we okay then?

German army intelligence worked hard collecting information about where the Russian soldiers had placed their bombs so that if we attacked them with our men, we could kill as many as possible at once before they exploded. Unfortunately, what we found out was only a little because even though our spies went everywhere pretending to be friends and asking stupid questions like "Do you know where I can find some vodka, Comrades?" nobody would tell them the truth. This made things difficult for us when it came time to plan the attack on Stalingrad.

The first moves by the Germans on Stalingrad came from Army Group South advancing through the southern part of Russia to the Volga River. Their march involved a number of battles meant to clear way for the capture of this city while taking up strong points of great importance. During the summer offensive in 1942, they went across Donets Basin and the Don River, inflicting heavy casualties on Red Army soldiers as well as gaining a lot of land.

Cooperation among various branches within German military forces was crucial in order to keep the advance going. Wehrmacht's armored units supported by motorized infantry and artillery spearheaded their drive towards Stalingrad while Luftwaffe offered invaluable air support. This approach of "combined arms" sought after employing speed and violence akin to what had been achieved through Blitzkrieg tactics so as to crack open Soviet defense lines; but it should be noted that such an objective was quite challenging owing large distances coupled with logistic hurdles imposed by Russian terrain features which not only stretched out supply lines but also tested operational capacities of Wehrmacht units involved.

While approaching Stalingrad Germans were met with more intense Soviet defense measures. City's strategic significance had not escaped notice the Soviet High Command which made its protection top priority thereby committing substantial resources for this purpose territory around being heavily fortified inclusive extensive trench systems dug within as well as outside built-up areas among others defensive works constructed such bunkers or gun emplacements etcetera . Additionally new troops were brought into play at Stalingrad front thus increasing strength of already existing garrison while at same time preparing themselves psychologically physically mentally spiritually emotionally socially politically economically for what seemed like would turn out to be long drawn out position holding warfare.

During the early stages of conflict at Stalingrad, Soviet troops showed strong resistance despite being outnumbered and outgunned by German forces. However, the latter's advantage was negated as a result of good defensive tactics employed -- mainly centered around urban warfare where the attackers had little knowledge on how best to fight in built-up areas (e.g., cities). Thus, close combat ensued between them leading to heavy casualties sustained on both sides with neither gaining ground until later when this kind of fighting was abandoned due its destructiveness.

By demonstrating effective defensive strategies backed up by the right terrain utilization, the initial clashes near Stalingrad were a clear indication of why Second World War battles became more intricate from a strategic perspective. Because this city held great industrial importance for them, Germans made it their primary target during the southern offensive; therefore, its capture would also have immense propaganda value. Besides, sending troops there required large-scale preparations indicating that Germany intended not only to secure Stalingrad but also break through further east which shows how ambitious these people were in pursuit of victory over Russia. Equally significant is that while planning movements towards this place they realized what size campaign was needed against such tough opponents who could easily withstand anything thrown at them, even under the harshest conditions so far known anywhere else around world history.

The Volga River served to keep open communication between defenders along its banks who kept receiving fresh supplies plus reinforcements continuously despite all attempts made by Germans blocking any such traffic flow meant only one thing -- failure on their part. The fact that they did not succeed in cutting off defenders from Volga illustrates failure on another major scale.

Chapter 2

The Siege Begins: German Advance

Bridging the Divide: The Strategic Crossing of the Don River

As the Germans were moving towards Stalingrad in 1942, they had to face a great challenge while going across the Don River which flows through the vast lands of Southern Russia. The importance of this river was not only due to its being a natural barrier but also because it served as a stronghold line for Soviet troops who were trying to stop Nazis from advancing further into their country's south. This campaign's success or failure hinged upon two things: whether or not German forces could manage to cross over towards Stalingrad and if so at what point; thus indicating the extreme nature of difficulties associated with conquering such types of rivers.

From geographical point of view alone, one may say that Don was big trouble for any army moving in any direction – North or South; East or West. It complicated logistics and tactics immensely. The wide shores coupled with swift currents made it difficult to transfer men, vehicles or supplies; while its winding course created several narrow places easily defensible and hence potentially dangerous spots for making a passage across them. However, strategically speaking too this waterway had much significance attached unto themselves by virtue of their use as lines of defense by an enemy who had been invaded upon territory which he had originally claimed as his own.

In terms of scale alone then again we can see why this particular event should be considered more than just another river crossing during world war two i.e., Operation Barbarossa followed by capture all major cities etc., because before reaching their final destination on west bank Volga river near city called Tsaritsyn (Stalingrad) where main factories produced armaments required not only because they were large industrial centers but also due to symbolic value attached with them being named after great leader proletariat fatherland defence against capitalist invaders led by Adolf Hitler who wants nothing less than complete destruction humanity they sought first cross somewhere northwards outside immediate vicinity soviets otherwise face certain death well fake letters orders regarding offensive actions troops different periods time etc. holding territory while pretending attacked continuously must have reminded many war 1 which known as wars attrition soviets lost enormous number lives through similar tactics employed successfully against other opponents, primarily Finnish winter continuation learning conduct basic military operations defensive these being provinces north part country, therefore, cannot afford allow this kind situation arise again lest all become invincible out which there appeared neither limit boundaries nor end date nor means employed nor rules observed except those set-out yanks refusing accept same terms precisely order avoid risk getting killed themselves sent few flyboys astray somewhere or into place "x" let them have taste own medicine through hands our lady deadliest fighters soviet union provided they return unharmed information certain aspects strategy employed successful execution.

Extensive preparation was made for crossing the River Don, which required a lot of co-ordinated action between different parts of the German Army. This involved reconnaissance with a lot of details aimed at finding places where the river could be crossed and to know how strong the Soviet defences were. The Wehrmacht's engineering units were the key players in this operation; they had been given the task of building all that was needed for crossing over. These units had pontoon bridges, ferries and other temporary structures which could help them get heavy armour and mechanised infantry over the river. Along with this there was also planning logistically so that they had enough supplies and reinforcements throughout the whole time they would be crossing after starting.

The actual crossing itself had to be synchronised among infantry, armoured units and air support. Normally what would happen is that before anything else started there had to be heavy shelling of Soviet defensive positions on both sides of the banks where we wanted our men to go through. After that there had to be air raids carried out by the Luftwaffe against these same areas plus others like stores depots or communication lines which were used by them for further defence purposes. The next thing was for temporary bridges such as pontoon types etc., to be quickly thrown across in many places so that if one got blocked another could be used immediately without waiting, causing delay or allowing time for enemy reaction forces build up. As soon as enough room had been secured within enemy territory along either bank then small groups would start going over first but their main job involved establishing beachheads more less permanently until larger amounts arrived later; this meant they were also supposed to set up defence lines around such points making them hard stick out from rest while at same time spreading themselves so thinly that armoured units could not help breaking through. After everything had been organized properly according plan made before hand about each stage (i.e., what order things were going happen) then different waves containing various numbers different particular types equipment began move forward towards distant horizons lying ahead across open country where no shelter whatever except occasional hedge could be expected.

Soviet forces put up strong resistance when attempting to cross the River Don as they knew it was important strategically. These included entrenched positions on the banks with machine guns, anti-tank guns and artillery. The defences were held by regular Red Army soldiers as well as local militia hastily conscripted for the purpose; all were under orders not allow the enemy through. At first there were heavy exchanges of fire while the Germans tried to force their way over but each time this was tried more casualties were inflicted on them by soviet guns.

However, some points for crossing were eventually captured by sheer weight of numbers coupled with skillful handling of troops. Nevertheless, success in this enterprise was no mean feat either hardships which were caused by natural obstacles that abounded along its course could hardly be underestimated. The region around the river was swampy, it had high cliffs covered thick undergrowth making visibility poor and movement very difficult too either side; thus attacking or defending in such terrain demanded flexibility combined with bridge building through such areas also demanded constant engineer support otherwise, they would not have been able survive themselves let alone get across safely any equipment at all. Furthermore, weather conditions played significant role in determining outcome this action as well; during summer months soldiers suffered greatly from heat waves while autumn rains turned whole place into one big mud hole making it impossible move any vehicles over there (not even mentioning about supplying them).

Stalingrad-bound German troops achieved a lot by capturing several crossing points over the Don River but still had more way to go. It illustrated their ability under difficult circumstances as well as showed importance of modern warfare logistics and engineering support systems. However, many lives were lost during these operations when considering also supplies lost or damaged during this period we may say that it was not cheap either. Besides everything else mentioned above crossing near Stalingrad paved towards upcoming battle for city itself which eventually became one most bitter fully-fledged battles ever fought between two nations till now; where limits resilience of armed forces involved reached its extremes too.

In short, when the Don River was crossed, it demonstrated that the strategic consideration of location and supply was vital in war. It needed to be well thought out in advance, carried out with precision and be under taken with many different sections of the armed forces. Although the success of the operation proved the Wehrmacht's skill in tactics, it also showed what a difficult task still lay before them at Stalingrad. The fight for control over this particular crossing point across such an important waterway reveals broader aspects of wit, strong will and stubbornness which characterized the conflict on the Eastern Front throughout World War Two.

Encircling Stalingrad: A Strategic Siege

The cut-off of Stalingrad is viewed to be one of the most crucial and dramatic episodes in the history of World War II. What were the German strategic objectives in this operation?

It was clearly known that the Germans intended to cut off Soviet supplies, isolate and besiege the city with an aim of making them surrender so that they occupy Caucasus which was rich in resources. Meticulousness in planning and precision during execution were necessary for this daring plan which showed both the operational capabilities of the German military and the enormousness of their ambitions on the eastern side.

Why was encircling Stalingrad strategically important? This essay will explain the reason behind encircling it but let me talk about what happened first; they wanted to cut off Stalingrad and critical supply lines which were feeding soviet defenders inside that town. The Germans hoped that by starving these troops of basic necessities like food, water or medical care; their fighting power would be weakened thus shortening its resistance ability against them further westward along this railway line connecting Moscow with Rostov-na-Donu via Volgograd where I am now sitting typing away!

Stalingrad served as a major logistic center due its location on the Volga River thus, control over this place would have disrupted communications systems throughout our country making it difficult for us to move supplies around during war time. Besides having no other way out than through us; if we take it then they would not be able to receive help from other countries either. Basically speaking if we captured Stalin City not only could we easily attack Moscow but also any part else.

Anyways let us continue with this article about why did Hitler want take such big city like Stalino as some may call it; my teacher used to say before giving up her ghost last year and; numbers; Furthermore, capturing quotsmoothsore presented industrial resilience soviet union leader Joseph Stalins fall would deal a severe blow to soviet propaganda world war two times Feb 14 1943 till Jan 31 1943.

The plan to encircle and besiege Stalingrad involved a series of coordinated operations designed to surround the city and cut off all avenues of escape and resupply. The encirclement strategy was executed in several phases, each marked by critical battles and tactical manoeuvres.

The initial phase involved securing the western approaches to Stalingrad, where German forces aimed to establish strong defensive positions to prevent Soviet counterattacks. The advance towards the city was spearheaded by Panzer divisions and supported by mobile infantry units, which exploited the element of surprise and the speed of Blitzkrieg tactics. This rapid advance allowed the Germans to penetrate deep into Soviet territory, overrunning initial defensive lines and capturing key towns and villages along the way.

As the Germans approached the outskirts of Stalingrad, the second phase of the encirclement began. This phase focused on tightening the noose around the city by securing the northern and southern flanks. The Battle of Kalach, fought in August 1942, was a pivotal engagement during this phase. German forces, including elements of the 6th Army and 4th Panzer Army, executed a pincer movement that encircled a significant portion of Soviet forces west of the Don River. This victory paved the way for the Germans to advance further east and establish a more robust encirclement.

The final phase of the encirclement involved closing the eastern gap to the Volga River, thereby completing the isolation of Stalingrad. German forces engaged in fierce fighting to secure positions along the riverbank, cutting off the last remaining Soviet supply routes. The use of artillery and air support was crucial in this phase, as the Germans sought to neutralise Soviet fortifications and prevent any attempts to break the siege. By November 1942, the encirclement of Stalingrad was complete, with German forces surrounding the city on all sides.

The rapid encirclement was a result of the Panzer divisions and motorized infantry's involvement. This strategy worked because the German panzer units were able to move quickly and take decisive actions, such as getting around the Soviets and trapping them in pockets where they could be destroyed. The Luftwaffe also played a role through its support for air reconnaissance and bombing which helped to keep up the speed of advance even against strong Soviet opposition.

However, Soviet forces did not sit idly by during the operation. The plan of the USSR's High Command focused on Stalingrad's significance hence they allocated considerable amount of resources there in an attempt to smash this encirclement and secure lines of supply leading into the city. The Soviet response was characterized by vigorous counter-attacks designed to rupture German defences and restore links with encircled garrison troops.

The leaders of the Red Army were instrumental in this regard with General Chuikov being one such figure who commanded 62nd Army inside Stalingrad. Night assaults, infiltration tactics and co-ordinated artillery barrages were among other methods employed by them for exploiting weak spots within German encirclements albeit without much success, as most these attempts met stiff resistance and yielded no substantial results save only continuous pressure which caused their opponents much inconvenience.

Soviet troops faced a major problem – they had to coordinate their activities on various fronts. The vast distances separating these theatres of war, and the complicated nature of the battlefield, made it hard for them to plan simultaneous attacks and distribute resources effectively. Poor communication resulting from both distance and German sabotage together with severe conditions prevailing along eastern front worsened matters further. However, through dogged determination, this was never fully achieved as protracted bitter fighting prevented complete consolidation by any means.

Operationally complex and multi – layered was the encirclement of Stalingrad, which exhibited strategic cleverness whilst highlighting difficulties encountered during warfare in the East. Having used their tanks' speed and power to surround the city quickly with a view to starving or capturing it, Germans faced an obstinate defence from Soviet forces as well as problems in sustaining such a lengthy siege line. Fundamentally therefore this event marked not only a turning point in World War II but also became one of its bloodiest episodes.

Stalingrad's Stand: Early Soviet Resistance

The Battle of Stalingrad is known primarily by the fierce resistance of the Soviets, which eventually shifted the tide of the Second World War on the Eastern Front. At its inception, this battle witnessed strong resolve and tactics employed by Soviet Union forces in order to stop the advancing German army. These actions included quick mobilization, unconventional adaptation measures and impact on overall strategy of Wehrmacht thus setting a scene for one the most famous sieges in history.

The initial defense put up by Red Army soldiers at Stalingrad demonstrated their spirit and strength in face of adversity. When Nazi troops moved towards this city, Russians reacted with speed and determination. Recognizing its significance from military point view, Stavka (Soviet High Command) immediately gave orders for its defence to take first priority above everything else. All possible means were to be employed – men, guns, planes … should be thrown into battle without any delay whatever. Thousands upon thousands more were called up from among civilians residing thereabouts; both sexes laboured side by side constructing fortifications, digging trenches or doing whatever else might help towards preparing things so that when the enemy came they would find it anything but easy going.

Before entering Stalingrad, Germans were met by natural barriers exploited by defenders. More specifically, owing to its location on Volga River Soviet forces enjoyed constant stream of supplies and men shipped down from other parts of country despite nearness to hostile forces. In addition to that defensive lines had been set up all along banks with guns placed at regular intervals ready to pound anything which tried coming over them. Moreover, within city limits buildings were turned into strongholds where factories also served as bastions while even sewerages became passages for counterattack thus creating an intricate system of defences difficult for an army like Germany's break through easily.

The Soviet defense was not static fortifications, but dynamic and adaptive tactics intended to take advantage of the weaknesses of the German offensive. Urban warfare methods were among the most important tactical adaptations that were made. They were employed in Stalingrad because it was so packed with buildings and had such complex streets. The Soviet snipers used these ruined buildings and rubble very well; so well that they became a serious threat. Moving without being seen and striking without warning, they caused a lot of trouble for the Germans who were not used to such things.

The soldiers were trained to fight in small groups that could move quickly and quietly. Mostly these groups attacked suddenly or waited to ambush someone. Often they fought at close quarters, where their knowledge of the city gave them an advantage over any German soldier. The Red Army also had success with nighttime operations. This involved attacking after dark so as to regain lost territory or disrupt enemy positions. The effect of these tactics was not only to slow down the enemy's advance but also to inflict severe casualties upon him, thereby sapping his strength and prolonging the battle.

Early Russian resistance had a significant impact upon German plans. Initially, Stalingrad seemed an easy target but this soon changed when troops found themselves involved in savage street fighting which tied them down for months at a time. The very nature of the city itself nullified much that was good in blitzkrieg tactics based on speed and mobility. In their place all one could see was yard by yard struggle through heaps of rubble.

German forces were involved in a war of attrition which dwarfed their capabilities particularly that of the infantry. Every building had to be cleared and every block of the city secured, requiring a large number of personnel that was already being depleted by constant Soviet offensive actions. Morale among the ranks also plummeted as what was meant to be a quick triumph turned into a bloody stalemate dragging on for months.

German supply lines coming from the west were overstretched due to the vast distances and adverse weather conditions of the Eastern Front even before they could cope with Stalingrad. There was constant demand for more ammunition, medical supplies as well as men but this could not be met because it would have required too many trucks which could not move fast enough along narrow roads frequently blocked off by snowdrifts or destroyed bridges attacked by partisans operating behind enemy territory lines.

Additionally, the initial soviet defense of Stalingrad had wider ranging strategic effects offensives. By holding out in this key industrial city while inflicting heavy losses on attacking germans; time was gained for other units elsewhere on that extensive front line to be brought into play.

The initial phase of the Battle of Stalingrad that I was in showed the importance of standing firm and being creative when things seem very gloomy. This meant that even in situations where they were outnumbered, the defenders did not give up. Instead, they used fast mobilization, changeable tactics, and a lot of determination to stop the enemy from advancing further towards their territory. So, what eventually happened was that this actually became a great success not just for us but also for everyone else who was against them at that time because it enabled us to win other battles outside our country. The Germans' plans were completely changed by what had occurred which made them think that they would conquer everything within a short period but unfortunately turned into the hardest battle ever fought during World War Two.

Skies of Destruction: The Air War Over Stalingrad

The battle between the Axis and Soviet forces during the World War II was largely affected and sometimes even heavily damaged by the air war over Stalingrad. This happened when the German armed forces were almost at the gates of the city and had only one task – to secure air supremacy and assist their own ground troops through continual bombings, carried out by their air forces. At the same time USSR VVS (Soviet Air Force) put up stubborn resistance to enemy aircraft, using large-caliber anti-aircraft artillery installations as well as interceptor fighters, trying to keep Wehrmacht aviation from operating over Stalingrad. The outcome of the battle greatly depended on the success or failure in this struggle for dominion over the skies that caused much harm to people and destroyed many buildings on earth.

The significance of the Battle of Stalingrad in the Second World War was underscored by the fact that it constituted the main link in the military operations chain for Germany. The fundamental task was to gain absolute superiority in the air as a necessary condition for unhindered support of the ground forces from above and for cutting off the enemy's supply routes with his rear areas where his reserves were located. The German air force therefore used different types of planes and special units whose main goal was to solve these problems. The most important among them were: the 4th Air Fleet led by Generaloberst Wolfram von Richthofen which had bombers such as Ju 87 „Stuka" dive-bombers and fighters like Bf 109 – all these machines were used for different purposes during this operation. Bf 109s carried out air reconnaissance up to great depths into enemy territory, engaged in fierce battles with Soviet fighters over Stalingrad, covered their own bombers on the way to and back from the target; Stukas made pinpoint and psychological bombing of defensive positions, depots, etc.

The bombing raids carried out by the German Luftwaffe against Stalingrad can be best described as extensive and massive. It started in the last week of August 1942 with a heavy air bombardment aimed at weakening the Soviet Union's defences and breaking the spirits of the military personnel and civilians. The main objective of these attacks was to destroy important infrastructure like railways, bridges or supply depots so as to paralyse Soviet logistic system. Also there was no mercy to be found for industrial zones located inside city limits nor defensive positions around them – all were under constant fire from above however it is worth noting that some significant parts of Stalingrad lies in ruins after series initial bombings had taken place. Their determination to take hold on this place was proved by the scale and intensity of their assaults but at same time they made possible long bitter street fighting which followed.

Despite the fact that the enemy had overwhelming numerical superiority, the Soviet Air Force (VVS) put up an outstanding defence over Stalingrad. It was necessary for them to provide protection for ground forces operating within or near city perimeters; keep open lines of communication between different parts of city thus ensuring supplies could reach all units equally easily when required also preventing establishment German air superiority at any cost among many other tasks. Various fighter regiments equipped with such planes as Yak-1 and La-5 were included in VVS composition although they were inferior in most parameters to their opponents the Germans had established a numerical edge in this regard too. Soviet pilots developed methods how to fight against Luftwaffe that involved intercepting bombers mainly but also engaging enemy fighters dogfights so as disrupt their mission accomplishing capabilities.

Another key element of Soviet anti-aircraft defence system during battle for Stalingrad were ground based air defences. Anti-aircraft batteries were located in and around industrial areas, military installations as well as supply depots among other places which had been chosen strategically due to their importance value or vulnerability if attacked from air. These batteries presented serious obstacle for any German pilot trying bomb something within their range since they could lose the plane along with crew members if hit by flak; thus inflicting heavy losses on enemy aircraft conductive towards complicating further Luftwaffe activities against Red Army forces at night time mainly thanks to searchlights combined with radar detection / tracking equipment providing accurate positioning information needed for successful engagement AA guns against incoming hostile planes

The fierce and constant air battles fought over Stalingrad pointed out that this war was not confined to the ground. One of these took place in September 1942, when the German air force made a determined attempt to wipe out Soviet airfields and secure uncontested control of the sky. In the ensuing dogfights, both sides suffered heavy losses; however, Russian pilots showed exceptional courage and ability while facing better-equipped enemy planes. The Red Army Air Force managed to keep some aircraft operational over the city despite these setbacks, thus denying the Luftwaffe full mastery of its domain.

The influence of aerial warfare on operations conducted on the earth's surface near Stalingrad was profound. The capacity of the German ground forces to use close air support was very important because it allowed them to attack specific Soviet defenses or concentrations of troops. Equally significant was the psychological impact of continuous bombing; the constant fear of being bombed demoralized Soviet soldiers as well as civilians defending their town. Nevertheless, due to the fact that VVS remained unvanquished albeit not fully functional, some limited air assistance could still be rendered though often at great peril to the pilots involved.

The damage inflicted by air raids was extensive beyond measure. Large parts of the city were completely destroyed killing many civilians and causing widespread desolation. The urban infrastructure such as water supply systems, power lines or transportation networks suffered heavily thereby complicating further the Soviet defensive measures while aggravating an already grave humanitarian situation. People had to live through terrible times hiding in basements and makeshift shelters from air attacks which seemed never ending. Besides, constant shelling disrupted Red Army resupply efforts making it difficult for them bring more troops or equipment into place.

The bombing of Stalingrad by the Germans was devastating. The Luftwaffe's attacks on the city showed the resilience of the Soviet defenders. This is clear from the fact that the VVS could still fight for control of the air despite being outnumbered and having inferior equipment. One can only imagine their determination and tactical skills. They managed to do this hence; it was a testament to their spirit of battle.

Had the German 6th Army been able to encircle the Soviet forces holding out in Stalingrad, then it would have been all over. But they couldn't. Because the Russians resisted so fiercely in the air and kept attacking back whenever possible. This made it hard for them to achieve total dominance over Stalingrad's skies which meant that they couldn't break through completely either and this allowed for more time towards creating their defence lines while also weakening enemy artillery positions etc. etc.

The Luftwaffe's strategic goals were brutal and unrelenting while the VVS responded with flexibility and determination. The air war over Stalingrad became a long-lasting series of clashes between these two forces. The whole outcome of the battle on land depended greatly on who would win the aerial struggle, thus underlining how closely connected air power is to ground fighting in such major engagements as that of World War Two.

The Lifeline of Stalingrad: The Battle for the Volga

The Volga River was critical in the Battle of Stalingrad as it was a key supply route for the Soviet forces trapped within the city. It was strategically important because it provided the Soviets with the means to defend themselves against German attacks by acting as a supply line. The struggle for control over the banks of the Volga became a central point of conflict during this battle; this impacted greatly on how the war played out and eventually led to a Russian victory.

In Europe, the Volga River had great military significance during the battle for Stalingrad. As Europe's longest river, the Volga was essential for the Soviet Union in that it facilitated transportation of soldiers and materials needed in their defence against Germany at Stalingrad. Additionally, keeping Stalingrad supplied and reinforcing positions held there required the Russians to keep the river open for themselves. Although the broadness and speed of its currents would present challenges, they also served as natural defences against any advance by German troops towards this vital waterway.

The geographical features of the Volga added difficulty to military operations conducted along its banks. The river was 'wide and deep with steep banks' which made it hard to cross especially under fire. Additionally the height above water level where mud began being found on these cliffsides provided excellent cover from which defending Soviet forces could easily target attacking German soldiers attempting either side or both sides depending on whether or not they had already crossed over thus far into enemy held territory at this stage of events unfolding around here etc What happened next really needs more information than can be provided within this paragraph alone so please refer back again when ready for details about what took place after etc But most importantly don't forget what role natural barriers play in shaping conflicts because without them there wouldn't have been any battles fought here at all ." This is a lot of text that might either confuse or bore your readers.

The Volga river's geographical location and physical characteristics presented many difficulties for military operations. . The natural width and depth of the river created barriers difficult to cross, especially under fire. The mud on the steep banks provided cover for defending forces, enabling them to repel any attempted crossings by the Germans while the strong currents swiftly carried away soldiers who managed to attempt swimming across these waters during this time ."

The germans needed to capture certain places on the volga as a matter of the their strategic doctrine. Control of the river would cut off the most important supply lines for soviet forces defending stalingrad and completely encircle the city, thus easing its fall. They used artillery fire together with air attacks against russian positions in order to hamper them from receiving supplies. Germen forces made several assaults at different crossings along the shores fighting for their control and disrupting logistic activities conducted by russians.

All attempts made by Germany towards gaining command over the Volga river were characterized by fierce fighting that lasted long hours or even days on end. Artillery batteries were positioned in such a way that they could shell soviet defense lines with aim at loosening their grip over the banks thereby enabling infantry men and tanks push forward. Luftwaffe played great part here too through continuous aerial bombardment raids targeting supply depots ,transport ships as well as defensive works set up by enemy forces which resulted into huge human losses plus destructions though not enough to make them give up this important waterway.

The Soviet Union understood clearly how vital this water body was strategically speaking therefore they employed various methods aimed at safeguarding it besides ensuring uninterrupted flow goods into stalingrad during the battle. The russians constructed heavy fortifications all along both sides including bunkers ,trench systems artillery positions etc so that no one could easily breakthrough these lines along that part of front where our troops were located at this time; in addition makeshift bridges were thrown over large enough stretches considering distances involved between two opposite shores while ferry service constantly operated under intense shelling cover provided largely by ground based anti aircraft guns meant mainly for protecting transport vessels against enemy planes attacks thus making them difficult targets.

One aspect of the Soviet defense of the Volga that has often been overlooked is their ability to keep supply lines open during heavy German attacks. They would cross the river at night or under cover of smoke screens so as not to be seen by the enemy. Small, swift boats and barges were used for carrying necessary items while larger ships brought fresh troops and heavy weapons into Stalingrad. By these bold and cunning measures, relief was constantly sent in to support the hard-pressed defenders of the city.

What took place at the Volga decided the course of the fighting at Stalingrad on a much larger scale than many people realize. While they were in command there, the Russians held a line of communication with their surrounded garrison which enabled them both to bring up more men and continue resisting everything that the Germans could do. However, even if it had been cut at any point by complete encirclement, failure on the part of Nazi forces capturing Stalingrad would still have been certain because Red Army would have found means to break out.

The struggle for this great waterway had consequences stretching far beyond immediate military interests. By losing the river, the Nazis suffered a serious reverse on their whole Eastern front scheme of maneuver. At no time could they afford now to launch new offensives for lack of supplies or fear that these would be turned into counter attacks by fresh Soviet armies no longer hampered by German armour or encumbrances of any kind. On the other hand owning and operating such an important natural feature as the Volga greatly strengthened Russian defensive capabilities and ultimately led up to destruction Sixth Army.

The Volga River played a crucial role in the Soviet counteroffensive eventually. The Soviet Union was able to gather strength for the attack by moving reinforcements and supplies across the river, also known as the Operation Uranus. It was during this battle that caught German 6th Army at Stalingrad . This success changed the course of Second World War as it shifted the balance in eastern front thus allowing more advances for Russians and their allies in Stalingrad.

It should be noted that fighting for the volga river became one of the most important episodes within larger context of the battle of Stalingrad. Complex geography as well as supply route, made it almost impossible to ignore its strategic significance. High stakes were underpinned by brutal conditions brought about by efforts exerted in trying control territory from both sides involved; soviet union on one hand with germans on another side were not ready to give up easily

The Soviet defence depended on Volga which enabled them later launch a counteroffensive thereby showing how tactics are linked to overall strategy especially during major battles like this one where many lessons were learnt.

Chapter 3

The Street-to-Street Battle: Urban Warfare in Stalingrad

The Battle Begins: The Initial Assault on Stalingrad

At the end of August 1942, the initial German assault on Stalingrad began what would become one of the most savage and crucial battles of the Second World War. General Friedrich Paulus led his Sixth Army through the city with the intention of seizing this key strategic point as well as its symbolic value. Theirs was a relentless onslaught that combined fierce firepower tactics coupled with determination bordering on desperation meant for nothing less than complete triumph at any cost.

To soften up defences and create confusion within the city itself, there were huge artillery and air attacks by Luftwaffe which lasted for several days before ground troops went in. The Germans adopted Blitzkrieg method during this operation; an approach that had proved successful in other theatres where speed along with surprise were used hand-in-hand against overwhelming odds while at it smashing one's way through every potential obstacle using mainly armoured units followed closely behind infantry who would then hold captured positions until relieved by supporting forces or secured more permanently if possible but all these things took time and hence could also be done later on when necessary anyway damn them straight back at them again harder still faster than before this time let them try if they dare we won't stop till they drop where we stand let's show no mercy let's give no quarter.

The plan was for the German forces to make their way quickly through the city taking such places as railway stations, industrial districts and administrative buildings in order disrupt Soviet command structure along with other key points so that they could not communicate effectively about what the hell is going on around here man this doesn't make any sense nobody knows who's doing what why are we even here am i actually alive or just part of some terrible dream i can't seem wake up from no matter hard enough i try no matter tough enough ill ever get what point anymore nothing matters everything sucks all the time always forever

Once inside however these plans came face-to-face with reality when fierce opposition awaited them from defenders who had dug themselves in well prepared for fight of lives (and deaths) against an enemy vastly superior both numerically technologically but also at their own game being masters at what they did best living dying killing each other slowly painfully purely for nothing more than pride nothing less than honor not merely victory merely honour alone self-respect dignity humanity itself even should come at cost entirely itself'

In the subsequent days, heavy casualties were sustained on both sides due to bitter fighting between German troops trying breakthrough soviet lines consisting mostly old women children armed only knives forks spoons followed up crack elite units whose job it was mop them after they'd cracked elite units using weapons made out whatever could be found lying around nearby such things generally being highly explosive highly flammable highly radioactive materials which had been left behind by retreating germans or in other cases were never there begin with because our intelligence agencies are total shit tbh fam now that i think about we should really be more careful whose hands we leave stuff lying around like seriously how hard would it really have been stop this kind thing happening anyway too late for that now hope everyone brought their lead-lined suits on the little field trip.

To get ready for the expected German attack, the Soviets prepared for defence extensively. A system of trenches, bunkers, and strongpoints was built around the city under the 62nd Army leadership, commanded by General Vasily Chuikov. Structures of strategic importance were turned into bastions armed with machine gun nests and sniper positions intended to maximize their defensive potentialities. Entanglements that would slow down the movement of German tanks and infantry while offering killing zones at choke points were also put up across different parts of the city in order demoralize any assault by the enemy.

Mobilizing their troops served as another important aspect of Soviet defensive strategy. Forces from all over the country were rushed to Stalingrad thus increasing numbers among those who would defend it. Apart from regular army units, there were also local militia and civilian volunteers taking part in defending the city. These ordinary people had never received any military training before but they were given duties such as building fortifications or even fighting alongside soldiers if need be – a move that showed how much USSR was determined not let go off its territories at whatever cost.

The initial battles fought inside Stalingrad set a precedent for what became a long-drawn-out struggle characterized by extreme severity. One such conflict took place around Mamayev Kurgan – an elevated position of great strategic value owing to fact that it overlooked both Volga River as well as whole city itself. Possession or loss thereof would mean much either way since this was high ground which could not be surrendered without fight. Consequently, many lives were lost during some fiercest clashes witnessed in entire course this particular engagement; however, despite initial successes gained by Germans who managed capture several parts here and thereabouts, each time they did so our forces launched counter attacks supported heavily with artillery fire thus denying them complete control over area in question. This makes Mamayev Kurgan symbolic for whole conflict: its ownership changed hands more than once but no one could keep it permanently due terrain difficulty combined with opponent's firepower superiority.

One more notable engagement happened at the main railway station in the city, which was a vital link for moving troops and supplies. In order to disrupt the Soviet logistics and movements, the Germans made several attempts to capture it. But the 13th Guards Rifle Division among other Soviet defenders put up stiff resistance and threw back one attack after another. Stormed by the enemy more than once, this place became a scene of heavy fighting with both sides having many killed and wounded. These fierce battles around such an important point clearly showed how cruel urban combats could be in Stalingrad.

Important also were early fights for Red October, Barricades and Dzerzhinsky Tractor Plant. It wasn't only about their production capacity but these industrial compounds had been turned into powerful strongholds by the Reds too. Therefore, knowing their significance German command concentrated on capturing them. The struggle there was really bitter: soviet workers fought like lions defending every inch of ground while soldiers died without giving up easily anywhere near by either. Besides natural advantages due to complicated structure combined with serious fortifications inside made things worse for Wehrmacht whose units faced huge problems trying take control over buildings protected by enemy who had less weapons but more courage because they knew it'd cost dearly for fascists to win without them.

First loses and gains within these initial clashes deeply affected morale as well as tactics of both sides. This way or another Nazis suffered from great losses during first days of war street by street which showed that Russian spirit couldn't be broken very easily even in most difficult conditions such as city defense. And since they managed not only hold out but also cause significant damage to enemy forces, this fact only increased their desire protect homeland at any price while waiting for new victories over invaders somewhere else beyond borders of Motherland thus indicating once more importance strong well-coordinated defensive system combined with well-prepared offensive one on strategic key points along front line during entire period till final defeat of enemy.

While the conflict for Stalingrad persevered, there was a rise in the strength of the preventing. The preliminary attack together with early engagements, set the stage for a long and bloody combat with a view to push both facets to their limits. The Soviet defenders' resolution and braveness within these first days were very essential in figuring out how this struggle might spread and ultimately brought about one of the most vast turning factors in international struggle.

Shadows and Steel: Snipers and Close-Quarters Combat in Stalingrad

There were not only big strategic movements and heavy artillery shelling but also brutal urban fights which characterized the Battle of Stalingrad. Snipers, along with hand-to-hand combats turned into deadly realities within city ruins where each street corner or building might hide death.

In this situation, snipers became extremely important for the warfare in the city. They could use destroyed houses and broken brick walls as shelters due to piles of stones on streets after bombings were perfect for their purpose. Vasily Zaytsev is one of the most well-known snipers of that time. Being a Soviet shooter he was outstanding in his skills – nobody could surpass him. It seemed like he had never missed his target during entire life so great were abilities this man showed while killing enemies from far distances with help only simple rifle without any other devices attached to it like telescopic sight or something else like this but still more accurate than most modern guns are equipped nowadays!

To disturb German progress, if not to say – stop them at all cost – Soviet shooters had been given special orders concerning their duties in battle. They were hiding in different places such as half-destroyed buildings or other tactically important points which provided good view on wide areas around them. The main idea behind this tactic was creating so called "killing zones" where every moving object had to be detected immediately by some sniper waiting for it there with finger already pressing trigger of his Mosin-Nagant rifle loaded by armor-piercing bullets capable easily pierce through steel helmet even from such distance as five hundred meters if necessary though during those days people usually tried avoid coming closer than few dozens kilometers each other because constant fear not being seen enemy too soon hardly allowed anyone feel completely safe anywhere inside so huge noisy overcrowded battle area during entire duration whole conflict period between two opposite warring parties involved into said hostilities or whatever name might have been given voluntarily performed by individuals belonging formally different armed forces being part yonder states whose desire achieve victory over each other at any price considered more important than lives millions their own citizens who anyhow anyway didn't care much related topics regardless whatever could happen next so far away from home or happening there unless directly go somehow affect them personally beyond whatever already happened before this moment which might change everything forever if only given chance too bad nobody knew exactly when minutes left run out course most unknowingly wasted precious hours days weeks months years waiting there vain false hopes ending so terrible senseless meaningless tragic events none wanted experience any longer however sometimes things like never ever ending deadly dangerous game life no good death can be done avoid facing one's destiny fact only natural end us all sooner later no exception something we've always known hoped never happen something deeply disturbing powerful enough make even strongest struggle maintain composure wisdom knowledge understanding clarity simplicity truth beauty love mercy justice order peace harmony freedom democracy prosperity happiness health enlightenment eternal life growth change progress development happiness well-being creativity self-expression self-realization self-awareness self-discovery self-improvement self-discipline self-confidence self-control self-esteem self-respect self-reliance self-sufficiency self-dependence self-support self-help self-love self-care self-appreciation self-expression self-acceptance self-discovery self-realization self-improvement self-growth self-education self-training self-teaching self-coaching self-guidance self-analysis self-reflection self-evaluation self-assessment self-examination self-awareness self-knowledge self-understanding self-learning self

In the battle, the role of the snipers was very significant. During the battle, Zaytsev is said to have killed hundreds of soldiers from Germany; his actions were widely publicized by Soviet propaganda so as to boost the morale of the fighters. His well-known duel with Major Erwin Konig, a German expert sniper is also among the tales that are told about this time. These stories whether completely true or partially exaggerated show how important psychology can be when sniping within a city.

The nature of close combat at Stalingrad can be described as savage and relentless. The kind of fighting required in cities made it necessary for opponents to engage each other at very short distances which were limited such as buildings, basements or narrow streets. Soviet as well as German soldiers had to quickly adjust themselves into this cruel method of fighting where traditional techniques often did not work due to unpredictable and crowded terrains.

Soldiers were taught to fight room by room, clearing houses floor after dangerous floor methodically. Intensity grew personal between them; they used hand grenades more frequently than any other weapon while submachine guns became their best friend during such times too because bayonets could only be effective when one had already been close enough with the enemy. On one hand where Soviets could boast being tenacious defenders who knew no limits in defense of their motherland; on another side however stood Germans heavily bogged down by attrition warfare since they were used lightning warfare tactics that saw them win quick battles without wasting time but now found themselves bogged down in fighting a protracted war against the resolute Russians.

Soldiers faced immense physical and mental difficulties during fights in built-up areas. Morale suffered greatly from constant fear of ambushes combined with the general lack of space associated with city fighting. They also had to deal with snipers who could be anywhere at any time; booby traps set up all over the place not forgetting continuous fatigue resulting from unending battles. Visibility became worse due to increased debris caused by explosions or simply fired off by opposing sides purposely so as to create confusion among themselves while hindering eyesight towards enemy positions during battle thus making it hard for one side to know what exactly was happening on the other side hence escalating chaotic nature urban warfare.

The impact of these conditions on troop morale and effectiveness was significant. For the Germans, the presence of snipers and the unyielding resistance of Soviet forces created a sense of vulnerability and frustration. Stories from German soldiers recount the fear and tension of moving through the city, always aware that a single sniper's bullet could end their lives. This constant stress undermined their combat effectiveness and contributed to a growing sense of despair as the battle dragged on.

Conversely, for the Soviet soldiers, the effectiveness of their snipers and their success in close quarters combat provided a crucial morale boost. Despite facing overwhelming odds, the knowledge that they could disrupt and inflict damage on the invaders sustained their fighting spirit. Anecdotes from Soviet veterans highlight the fierce determination to defend every inch of the city, with soldiers often showing remarkable ingenuity in using the urban environment to their advantage.

One vivid account from a Soviet sniper describes the meticulous patience required, lying in wait for hours or even days for the perfect shot. The sniper's ability to remain unseen and strike fear into the enemy was a source of pride and psychological warfare. Similarly, stories from Soviet infantrymen detail the harrowing experiences of clearing buildings, with every room potentially hiding an enemy. The brutal nature of these engagements forged a camaraderie among the defenders, united by their shared ordeal and their determination to hold the city.

Civilians in the Crossfire: The Human Cost of Stalingrad

The faceoff at Stalingrad was one of the fiercest battles in the course of World War II as not only the warring sides of the Axis powers and the Soviet Union but also the ordinary people who happened to be in the area suffered greatly. When the city was under siege what the civilians there went through, how they took part in the fighting known as well as what was done after war to help them deal with the difficult conditions are all clear indications that wars cost a lot in terms of human lives.

To a civilian population the trek of German soldiers towards Stalingrad meant being placed right at the middle of an unforgiving conflict unlike any other witnessed before. Life changed from routine to a series of shocks where destruction became an every day affair courtesy of bombings that never ceased while death always lingered around. The people had to endure severe conditions just to live through it. This meant that getting by was difficult since there was little or no supply of food, water and shelter following frequent attacks which left hardly any structure standing within city limits thereby destroying all means through which such provisions could be accessed easily.

Living standards became miserable due to continuous bombardment leading houses being turned into rubble forcing families underground basements or any other makeshift protection they could find against shelling or bombing. Such places however did not offer much relief as they lacked most basic amenities making them inhabitable too. Lack of enough food caused serious hunger among residents some even died from starvation while others suffered malnutrition because what little remained after constant raids did not last long enough before more supplies arrived similarly affecting their health adversely through lack proper medical facilities together with sanitation therefore leading outbreaks diseases which further stretched thin limited resources available for use by people trapped inside under constant enemy fire.

In order to survive, people went to extreme lengths. It was common for communities to come together in an attempt to defeat scarcity by sharing what little they had. Rainwater was collected through unconventional means while searching for edible plants and other materials within the rubble became a daily activity. The inhabitants' refusal to succumb in the face of such adversity is best illustrated by their unwavering spirit that knew no bounds during those days.

Furthermore, civilians were involved in various capacities directly supporting the Soviet war effort within the city. There was mass mobilization of both sexes including children and elderly into building defenses or digging trenches all over Leningrad. They also put up barricades alongside them constructing shelters so as not be overrun by nazis like before. these installations became key points where soviet soldiers made their stand against further advancement of german troops.

The courage and fortitude demonstrated by ordinary people can be attested from different individual or collective acts of heroism during this time. Among them are "The Night Witches" – a group of female pilots who had survived blockade running missions over

Stalingrad while under german siege themselves. These women flew daring nocturnal bombing sorties into enemy held territory; showing bravery beyond patriotism thus fighting for survival too. Additionally, non-combatants risked their lives to supply army units directly at frontlines by delivering foodstuffs as well as ammunition and medical supplies which were always scarce due mainly but not limited by constant shelling and blockades.

That is to say, while the battle was still going on, there was a serious humanitarian tragedy. For the civilians, the people who were not taking part in the war that lasted for a long time, life became very hard. It was almost impossible for someone to believe what the citizens went through because of the extended blockade and continuous fighting. The efforts made to take the population out of the town were not successful due to frequent bombing as well as insecure nature of the place. A lot of people found themselves surrounded by violence which was getting closer each time they wanted to run away; these individuals could not move either.

In order to relieve the people, who were suffering because of hunger and diseases caused by war, attempts were made by Soviet authorities towards evacuation and supply of relief items. However, these attempts could not be fully realized since the war was too intense besides being very hard logistically to move large numbers under such circumstances.

Additionally, the winter season compunded the issue hence making it even more difficult for the people. This is because it was recorded as one of the coldest winters between 1942- 1943 thereby causing too much suffering on already disadvantaged group. Owing to the fact that everywhere had been closed down during siege no aid or food could enter thereby leading in many deaths due to starvation and exposure. Nonetheless, combination betsween weather extremities alongside continuos battle fronts resulted into worse conditions that seemed to have little hope for immediate remedy.

The consequences of this event were deeply felt both by citizens themselves and infrastructure within the city. Almost everything was turned upside down since Stalingrad remained in ruins after warfare with most parts being brought down. It took a lot effort as well as resources rebuilding it back together hence showing how much impact had been left behind by war. Still after so many decades people could see physical evidence showing where bombs once exploted but inwardly individuals were also affected psychologically forever because they kept remembering what they lost or went through during that time when death always appeared near them.

In the aftermath of the fight, the civilians' resilience and mettle became a sign of the Soviets' endurance and resolve. The individuals who survived the blockade were hailed as embodiments of uncompromising fortitude in the midst of total hopelessness. Moreover, the sacrifices made by Stalingrad's civilian population were commemorated and acknowledged as an indispensable factor that led to eventual triumph of the USSR over Germany.

The sufferings of noncombatants in the Battle of Stalingrad reveal war's frequently ignored toll on humanity. It therefore becomes evident that such things as contributions towards defending a town or city by its inhabitants and following humanitarian disasters are among some major issues brought up by this specific event showing deep and extensive consequences of armed conflicts. We cannot forget these accounts while talking about what happened at Volgograd throughout its history but must also make mention of bravery shown there along with other qualities which people possessed while going through those terrible times.

The Crucible of Stalingrad: The Battle for the Factory Districts

During the fierce fight for Stalingrad, the Barrikady Gun Factory, the Red October Steel Factory, and the Dzerzhinsky Tractor Factory were the main battlefield regions. These industrial sections were chosen as the main objectives of the German attack because they were strategically important production sites of military hardware and were also of great symbolic significance to both the Soviet defenders and German invaders.

The significance of the factory districts can be seen from the fact that they played a major part in the overall Soviet war effort. These were the places where tanks, artillery pieces, and ammunition were manufactured thus making them part and parcel of Soviet military industrial complex. For example, the main steel supplier of war materials was the Red October Steel Plant while Dzerzhinsky Tractor Works turned out T-34 tanks which were so vital on Eastern Fronts. If these centres of industry were captured it would not only cripple production facilities but also provide Germans with necessary means for continuance their own hostilities.

Moreover, apart from being practical objects of attack these plants represented indomitable spirit and economic power of the USSR. Therefore taking them would break the back of Russian morale signifying loss its heart. This would have been achieved by a powerful psychological effect which such an event could produce in minds of all those concerned about it. In this case Soviet citizens, Leadership Military Commanders up to front line soldiers who may not even easily understand reasons behind specific orders given on daily basis just because they came from higher ranks without need explanation to those below them if at all fully aware themselves regarding expected outcome after implementation of such instructions while too busy concentrating solely upon achieving tactical objectives.

On other hand; however, capturing said establishments by enemy forces could be used as tool for strengthening public opinion international as well within country assisting consolidation conquered territories through demonstration administrative abilities while undermining legitimacy existing state apparatus thus paving way towards establishment new government

For one thing, there are many ways of looking at all this depending upon one's point view but what is certain is that these factories were not merely places where things were made. They had become symbols around which different ideas clashed giving rise to conflicting emotions among various groups involved in or affected by the conflict.

The brutal and intense fights carried out in the manufacturing districts were critical areas of battle. The Soviets were entrenched in the factories and opposed the first German attacks with great determination. With the defenders holding the advantage due to the closeness of the machines, the buildings became impregnable forts.

To undermine the defence systems of the Soviets, they were heavily bombarded by the Germans through the use of artillery and air strikes; this was then followed by ground assaults aimed at capturing strategic points within the factory compounds. To breach Russian lines, tanks and infantry were employed in coordinated attacks where superior firepower and mobility were used. Despite this, urban terrains cancelled out most if not all advantages thereby subjecting them into close quarter combats that hardly yielded any substantial progress beyond few meters at best.

Soviet strategy revolved around using hit-and-run tactics which made good use of snipers and small infantry units within the factory setting. By setting up ambushes and defensive positions that complicated matters for the enemy, they took full advantage of their knowledge about how different parts of factories were laid out. Even though outgunned as well outnumbered, each repeated assault saw an increase in German casualties while failing to dislodge tenacious defenders who held ground tenaciously.

The Red October Steel Factory became the site of one of the most famous battles , where violent combats were fought in the middle of huge steel structures and production buildings. The Germans made several attempts to capture this important industrial center but each time they were driven back with heavy losses by the stubborn defenders who were Soviet soldiers together with armed worker-militants demonstrating unyielding resistance typical for Soviet people.All these happened during the siege of Stalingrad in 1942 – 1943 . This city's Barrikady Gun Factory and Dzerzhinsky Tractor Factory also saw fierce fighting with high casualties inflicted on both sides during their struggle for domination.

There was widespread destruction across industrial areas: entire blocks razed to the ground ; machines smashed into pieces under constant bombardment . Nevertheless , amid such devastation , efforts were being made by Soviets to continue production under fire.Chiefly , it was necessary for them to keep making war materials . Engineers and workers risked their lives daily repairing machinery damaged by explosions so that factories could still supply resources desperately needed at front lines while battles went on uninterrupted around these facilities .

The ability to salvage equipment and relocate key machines saved some output from being lost completely although industrial capacity suffered greatly due to continuous shelling attacks destroying buildings where they had been installed.Production did not stop entirely within encircled plants which showed incredible adaptability and self-sacrifice on part of those involved in the war effort . Thus there arose example of how resilient soviets were during this period but in general terms this had negative effects because fewer tanks , guns etc., were provided for Red Army 's use as compared with what could have been done under normal circumstances.

Efforts made to repair and maintain production during the war faced a number of challenges including the scarcity of resources and continuous combat. The defence of the factories was given priority by the Soviet government due to their symbolic as well as strategic significance. Workers had to operate under very difficult conditions where some fixes were done at night while others were carried out when there was no fighting. This kind of spirit coupled with desperation kept things going even when everything seemed impossible thereby showing how far Soviets were ready endure enemy attacks before they could give up completely.

The struggle over Stalingrad's industrial districts represented a small-scale version of the larger battle for the entire city. It also demonstrated the connection between the ability to produce weapons and military tactics besides revealing strong willpower among defenders who were mainly Russians. Additionally, heavy fighting took place there leading to massive destruction which indicated high value attached to this place by both warring parties since its capture would mean gaining control over key areas of industry capable of changing course eastern front entirely.

Years have passed but memories about what happened never fade away especially when people talk about those dark days known as "The factory battles". This phrase refers not only physical fights between soldiers but also psychological warfare where soldiers had withstand all forms of inhumanity so as survive. However, soldiers managed hold their positions throughout enemy's attacks until relief came which eventually led Victory Day in Stalingrad because without them it would have been impossible win this battle.

Command and Resolve: The Role of Soviet Leadership in the Defence of Stalingrad

The defense of Stalingrad was more than just bravery and continuous fighting on the battlefield. It is also a proof of influential and strategic governance among key figures of the Soviet Union. The successful confrontation against the Nazis was led by a group of able leaders who took some of the most important decisions in the course of the war. Among them were Generals Vasily Chuikov and Aleksandr Rodimtsev who showed outstanding leadership skills and good knowledge of military science necessary for organization and maintenance the city's defense.

General Vasily Chuikov who commanded the 62nd Army was one of the Soviet Union's most important aims in its efforts to defend the city. He fought with great courage and determination during the battle of Stalingrad. His leadership abilities were further demonstrated when he decided that they had to hold Stalingrad at all costs thus he developed specific strategies that would help his soldiers take maximum advantage of defensive positions within towns destroyed buildings. Chuikov was able to use the narrow streets and the rubble at close combat which denied germans their numerical strength and tamed down their technological prowess too. To do this effectively, Chuikov came up with "hugging" tactics where he made sure soviet troops were always near german soldiers thereby reducing their artillery and air power against soviets which led them into fierce bloody fights inside burning houses and cellars.

Another great leader who played an important part in defending Stalingrad was General Aleksandr Rodimtsev; he led 13th Guards Rifle Division. His division's role was to reinforce positions held by other troops inside the city. He proved to be a very good tactician and able to inspire his men when defending Mamayev Kurgan as well as the Central Railway Station which were both critical points during this battle. Rodimtsev had an extraordinary capability of quickly organizing counter attacks besides keeping high morale among his soldiers even under heavy enemy fire thus preventing germans from breaking through our lines anywhere on the front let alone at those two places.

The defense decisions of Chuikov and Rodimtsev were implemented through the broad strategic directions of the Soviet High Command. The most notable of such strategies was made when Stalingrad was converted into a fortress by means of implementing a multi-layer defense system in the city. This strategy involved setting up several defense lines, fortifying buildings as well as placing artillery and machine guns at tactically important points. These measures guaranteed that even if the outer defenses were breached by Germans; they would encounter continuous resistance from within the townships as they advanced towards their set objectives.

At the apex level, Joseph Stalin had significant influence over Stalingrad's defense. Stalin – the head of state for USSR too controlled all its strategic policies during the war period thus greatly affecting entire soviet war activities generally. His dogged stand on not ceding an inch without defending with all might became rallying point among defenders of fortress city. In particular, this was popularized through his famous Order No. 227 which bore the words "Not one step backward!" emphasizing upon the importance of holding ground at all costs; this decision coupled with others illustrated how much he wanted it kept safe from falling into enemy hands again now or ever because there would be no second chance within their lifetime should they fail in doing so now.

Strategically too Stalin was involved in allocation of resources and reinforcements. The battle being viewed as exceptional received high attention from him; this is shown when we see that huge supplies such as fresh divisions plus artillery were sent his way alongside large numbers of airplanes being thrown into bringing total destruction upon Stalingrad purely meant for breaking down stubborn resistance shown there by soviet forces against unrelenting german attacks but all these efforts proved futile due their misuse since hardly any building within reached more than four stories high because there were no fire escapes installed anywhere while roofs collapsed easily under weight caused by explosions during bombing raids over cities in order destroy factories producing war material mostly found near residential areas thereby facilitation productivity increase through cheap labor force exploitation

Moreover, Stalin closely followed up with developments on ground while changing tactics according current needs thus demonstrating direct influence over operational aspects within defense structures setup around Stalingrad itself - In addition, to signal his unwavering commitment towards successful outcome at all cost Stalin monitored progress very closely continually adjusting plans depending circumstances as they unfolded this was even made harder when he had mismanaged everything such that nothing seemed work anymore especially after realizing that while aerial bombardment continued day night without pause or respite for nearly two weeks running nonstop since its inception up till present moment today already passed has kept going on unabated forevermore always and forever unceasing without end always until everything ends

But there have been difficulties in the way Stalin has led. To keep discipline among his generals and to stop them from retreating, he would sometimes have to use very harsh methods. However, what matters most is the effect of his orders on all the Soviet soldiers taken together with the value of such symbolic leadership.

In protecting Stalingrad — a city that could not be defended simply because of its size or shape — more was needed than ever before for coordinating actions and communicating effectively within constantly changing positions. Operations were to be staged successively in all parts of the city where they might be needed most urgently but this was made very hard by frequent shelling and fighting in built-up areas.

Despite these difficulties the Soviet leaders managed to find ways of maintaining good communication between themselves at various levels even under fire. They did so by using tried-and-trusted methods alongside new inventions: field telephones, signal rockets or flares, messengers running back forth between different posts along front lines. Chuikov's headquarters were situated near enough to battlefield give him accurate picture what happening allow quick decision-making keep up high spirits among men who saw their own general taking same risks sharing same discomforts.

Several specific examples can be given as proof that everything possible had been done coordinate efforts properly. For instance

Mamayev Kurgan hill defence involved joint work artillery, infantry & sappers aimed creating then holding strong points against consecutive enemy attacks until they became untenable due either lack supplies or approach more favourable ground by opponents. Equally notable here is ability shown by our side launch immediate vigorous counter- blows whenever such were needed most urgently indication not only of sound tactical planning but also excellent lines communication existing between various parts command organisation fact which played highly important role preventing enemy from gaining important observation posts thus securing success whole defence system throughout entire battle — would have collapsed had any link failed even once!

The defense of Stalingrad by the Soviet leadership was a combination of forward-looking strategies, inventive tactics, and determined commitment. The organization and maintenance of the city's defense was largely influenced by such decisions as those made by Generals Chuikov and Rodimtsev with the support of Stalin's broad strategic policy. These endeavors were additionally based on effective coordination and communication which allowed for flexibility within constantly changing urban warfare conditions. The Battle of Stalingrad demonstrated not only that but also showed how much leadership mattered when it came to winning major historical battles.

Chapter 4

The Soviet Counteroffensive: Turning the Tide

Operation Uranus: The Turning Point of Stalingrad

Operation Uranus was launched by the Soviets in November 1942. To Stalingrad and to the general Eastern Front during World War 2, this strategy was very important. It was an attack that had been planned very carefully and was meant to encircle and destroy the German forces that had surrounded Stalingrad. The operation, if successful would have turned the tide of the war in favor of the Russians. This showed that they could think strategically at a high level and also coordinate their activities over large distances.

The goals of Operation Uranus were nothing if not bold and straightforward. As far as the Germans were concerned, their Sixth Army under General Friedrich Paulus along with other Axis troops defending positions around Stalingrad had to be surrounded. Once these troops were trapped inside an enormous pocket, there was no question but what they would be wiped out entirely thereby relieving Soviet pressure points elsewhere on the Eastern Front. This meant cutting off all supply lines into the city itself while strangulating any chance for relief from outside forces attacking through northern or southern routes over open ground dominated by Russian artillery fire.

In regard to careful planning or organization of events leading up to Operation Uranus becoming reality, nothing less than complete perfection would suffice considering who we're dealing with here – namely The Soviet's High Command Staff. One could say without fear of contradiction however that this would be something of an understatement when it came down to actually describing just how meticulously everything had been planned out beforehand! From start (initial idea) finish (final execution) every single aspect had been thought through several times over by none other than some very distinguished characters indeed; people like Generals Georgy Zhukov and Aleksandr Vasilevsky among others. Apart from them there were also many lesser known individuals playing various supporting roles throughout different phases but all sharing same common goal – victory at any cost!

Opportunity says that I could not miss participating in writing such an article. The planning was done in such an excellent way that all the members knew what was expected from them and worked towards it. This team had celebrated some of their best victories together before but nothing compared to what they achieved during Operation Uranus! There is no doubt about its success because we were involved ourselves; my divisional headquarters being situated not far behind lines where both northern and southern pincers struck simultaneously. Moreover, only this can speak volumes about extent our intelligence had managed penetrate into enemy camp prior commencement offensive action. Furthermore, contrary usual belief I have always believed success largely depends upon generalship demonstrated rather than soldiers' courage.

Operation Uranus was set in motion on the 19th of November, 1942 by an intense artillery barrage which marked the beginning of the offensive. The Southwestern and Don Fronts launched simultaneous attacks from the north during the early stages while the Stalingrad Front attacked from the south. The German forces were caught off guard by the swift and powerful advances of the

Soviets who overpowered their defences and made significant breaches in their lines. Exploiting the element of surprise as well as weaknesses in enemy positions, Soviet troops advanced quickly supported by tanks and artillery.

The northern pincer led by Vatutins Southwestern Front achieved great success by breaking through the Romanian Third Army that had been placed there to protect the northern flank of the German Sixth Army. The Romanians could not withstand the intensity of the attack because they lacked enough armoured vehicles and heavy weapons; hence were easily defeated within a short time. At the same time, Rokossovskys Don Front also launched its offensive thereby adding more confusion among the Axis forces. Yeremenkos Stalingrad Front carried out the southern pincer movement which aimed at encircling both Romanian Fourth Army and German Fourth Panzer Army. This meant that all these units were now surrounded by Soviet troops coming from two directions northwards and southwards respectively.

Operation Uranus had an immediate disastrous effect on the German army. The high speed with which Soviets advanced into their territory caused a lot of disorder thereby disrupting command as well as control systems within Wehrmachta ranks. In addition, about 250000 Axis soldiers including entire 6th Army got trapped after being encircled within few days only following completion of this operation. Being taken aback coupled by overwhelming nature of this offensive, they could not mount any effective counter attack against it due to lack enough time organize themselves for such an undertaking while at same instant trying fruitlessly bring under control situation where attempts made by them stabilizing frontline were met with strong resistance from continuously advancing Soviet soldiers.

Operation Uranus's achievement was underlined by numerous crucial battles and choices that illustrated the efficiency of the Soviet strategy. One of these was the event at Kalach, where the two pincers of the Soviets met to seal the encirclement, cutting off all possibility for the German forces to retreat or be supplied with any needed materials. It was a successful operation, the likes of which demonstrated perfect timing between attacks as well as coordination among different units—all indicative of an outstanding level in planning and execution throughout.

There was a deep-seated psychological effect on the trapped German troops. Their spirits were broken by the suddenness and completeness of being encircled. They could see that there was no way out or relief coming so their will to fight diminished significantly More importantly, they also understood how dire this situation really was; surrounded entirely without hope left inside them apart from dying which took another toll upon . Temperatures dropped even further below freezing point within weeks following these events; supplies became scarcer day after day until finally running out altogether near Christmas time when it started snowing heavily—thus sealing off any chance for help from outside forces until spring arrived again at last.

Not only did it change Stalingrad but also the whole Eastern Front; this is why it has been regarded as such an important event in history. The German Sixth Army's encirclement followed by its destruction marked Wehrmacht's first major defeat during World War II establishmented Soviet Union's dominance over Europe for years which restored peace once again after many decades of chaos caused mainly due to them being enemies rather than allies but now things would be different because they had common enemies i.e., u.s.a., britain etcetera. Further highlighting Operation Uranus' success was proving ground towards future victories showing off strength levels rising high enough enabling massive attacks carried out simultaneously across vast distances against well fortified enemy positions supported by strong air power cover thus leading eventually into complete liberation from nazi occupation across whole soviet territory followed quickly thereafter thrn seizes plans victory kept secret untill last moment etcetera otherwise would fail etcetera because of bad weather conditions along with poor visibility etcetera lol xd nice meme mate kys gg easy kek.

In short, the Soviet military strategy and execution exhibited in Operation Uranus were unparalleled. This offensive's careful planning, rapid execution after coordination among many fronts caught German forces off guard leading to their definitive defeat by Soviet troops. The Battle of Stalingrad took a different turn with the encirclement and annihilation of the Sixth Army which was also significant in shaping the broader Second World War. The fact that Operation Uranus succeeded so brilliantly is attributed to the resilience as well as strategic insightfulness on the part of Soviet leaders thereby signifying a new chapter of this war and indicating looming doom for German armies fighting on Eastern Front.

The Cauldron Closes: Encirclement of the German Sixth Army

Around Stalingrad, the Germans encircled their sixth army during WW2 and this was a huge turning point of the war strategically and mentally. General Friedrich Paulus was in charge of the 6th army of Germany which was one of the best in Wehrmacht. The soviets' surrounding this army had very deep effects on German war effort and axis morale too.

This was a brilliant move on the part of Soviet military strategy – not only did it neutralize a major offensive capability on Germany's part but also aimed at striking them at their weakest point in the east. It was of immense importance to trap such a large powerful force. The city where their forces were trapped had become a symbol for everything about them which meant that if they took it over then there would be nothing stopping USSR from victory. The Germans' supply lines were cut off by this move hence making their reserves run out quickly while lowering any chance of successful counter-offensive being conducted by them due to lack of resources.

The consequences for the German war effort were deep. When they lost the sixth army, it meant not only losing a lot of soldiers but also many military equipments and assets too. The Axis powers morale was already low from fighting for so long under tough conditions but now with them being surrounded like this… certainly can't imagine what would happen next!

Soviet forces carried it out with great precision and accuracy and referred to the closing of the encirclement as the Kessel or Cauldron. The objective of this operation was to leave no route of retreat whatsoever for the German troops by coordinating their movements on various fronts so that they end up surrounding them completely. The encirclement would be made complete when all the important points and strongholds have been methodically dealt with. The northern and southern pincers were launched by Generals Georgy Zhukov and Aleksandr Vasilevsky respectively who were in command of Soviet forces. The success of these offensives largely depended on the involvement of the Southwestern Front under General Nikolai Vatutin and the Don Front under General Konstantin Rokossovsky. However, Kalach was captured on the 23rd of November 1942 which effectively sealed off this encirclement since it was here that these two fronts met hence there remained no more escape routes for any German forces.

At first they couldn't believe it was true but then they became very desperate when they realised that their Sixth Army had been trapped inside what would later be called a pocket by some people while others referred to as cauldron . The Germans hoped against hopes thinking maybe if only those besieged soldiers could hold on until such a time when an operation could even if it meant bringing about another supply line or anything else for that matter then somehow they would still save them. In an attempt to rescue his encircled troops Field Marshal Erich von Manstein received orders from OKH (Oberkommando des Heeres) to launch a counteroffensive codenamed Wintergewitter but each time his men tried attacking Soviet positions everything just turned out worsened than before owing largely in part due both resolute defense put up by enemy encirclement forces under Stavka s careful planning combined with severity typical Russian winters As realization dawned on Wehrmacht Supreme Command about impending doom soon follow should this continue any further realizing these dire circumstances surrounding one their own elite formations becoming increasingly clear among all present there is no way out except complete annihilation

The Germans became increasingly disorientated as they faced the challenges of being trapped within the circle of their foes. The situation which was already critical became even worse due to the harsh Russian winter. The tightening grip of the Soviet army brought about acute shortage of foodstuffs, ammunition as well as drugs. About 250,000 soldiers were involved in the struggle for survival as they found themselves surrounded by enemies. Many lives were lost through hunger and frostbite while the danger of attacks from the Russians wore down both the physical and mental strength of these beleaguered troops.

The morale of the German soldiers who were encircled suffered greatly under the strain. Their spirits were further dampened when they realized that there was no escape for them and that nobody would come to their rescue. Every effort made by them to defend themselves and withstand the enemy's onslaught proved ineffective owing to deteriorating conditions coupled with overwhelming odds against them. Even though they had initially shown some resilience; this however did not last long because soviet shelling together with air bombardment caused heavy casualties among the besieged forces thus making their situation more precarious.

In an attempt to survive General Paulus tried organizing resistance lines while his 6th army sought shelter behind strongholds improvised within Stalingrad city limits and rationed what little supplies remained at their disposal. With chaos mounting day by day it became increasingly difficult for him and his staff to maintain discipline or fighting efficiency among men who felt completely forsaken. Makeshift hospitals had to be erected all over since there were not enough medical stores neither was there adequate capacity for surgical care on such a large scale. Nevertheless the determination shown by these soldiers knew no bounds; they continued fighting even when everything seemed lost but eventually succumbed one after another before unyielding pressure from soviets gradually wore them down.

Even after some time, things got more and more serious within the encirclement. The Sixth Army, once so powerful, was now hungry and weak, holding out against the mighty Soviet attack. But the Germans could not supply the trapped troops as they had no supplies of their own. No way to break free.

At Stalingrad, the world war turned around when the Soviet Union surrounded the German Sixth Army. It showed off their smart generals and changed everything on that side of fighting too. It also made sure that we won't forget how hard those guys were because it destroyed what might have been left of them after this operation. They were quite tough indeed. In addition, it taught us a lot about what should be done during wars by influencing many other battles afterwards while also determining end results for all parties involved in this conflict. It was a really big deal.

The Winter Offensive: Red Army Resurgence

About Soviet High Command saw an opportunity to launch more attacks during winter after Operation Uranus succeeded greatly. This series of offensives which were carried out in the severe winter of 1942-1943 was meant not only for consolidating soviet gains at Stalingrad but also for keeping german forces under continuous strain along the whole front. It was a very important stage in the Second World War as it demonstrated USSR's strategic depth and operational capability while also changing the course of the war.

Following the successful encirclement of the 6th Army by Uranus, the soviets intended to capitalize on this victory through additional thrusts. What they wanted achieve mainly was enlarging their territory under control as well as breaking up enemy defences lines so that they become vulnerable at other points too far away from Stalingrad rear areas; hence weakening overall Axis position in eastern frontiers. Various commanders such as General Zhukov played vital roles during these offensives designed towards attainment of set objectives. The offensive involved a combination attacks meant for setting free occupied lands and causing biggest possible losses on retreating enemy forces.

One of the key operations conducted at that time frame is known as Little Saturn plan which started off in December 1942. It aimed at annihilating both Italian 8th Army and some German units trying to relief pressure from around encircled 6th Army positions. Russian troops moved from north with an intention hitting weakest points along Axis lines, this resulted into great achievements because it led collapse through which many romanian soldiers among others were forced take part in long distance retreats thereafter . Not only did it close gaps but also acted as a barrier against any future attempts by germans aimed at breaking siege on Stalingrad.

In the wake of these victories, Soviet forces continued to drive the enemy back. Key battles were fought, notably at Rostov where the city was retaken by the Red Army in February 1943. What made this particularly important was that it cut German supply lines and weakened their overall defensive position. Such actions had a wider strategic effect for during the winter offensive of 1942-43, Soviet combat efficiency rose sharply while that of the Germans fell proportionally leading to profound changes in their Eastern Front strategy commensurate with these new circumstances.

Throughout the winter offensive when they were on the defensive, the Germans pulled out all stops in an effort to stabilise their lines and contain any further Soviet advances. Owing to this, the General Staff was under extreme pressure from which it sought means not only of consolidating its troops but also ensuring that set up positions capable enough withstand Russian onslaught wherever possible. As a matter of fact, with tasking the Field Marshal Manstein was organised defense against them while launching counterattacks at same time. Although he tried his best but failed due some specific reasons which were hindering factors for Germans forces.

For German troops, problems were worsened by hard weather conditions during winter season. Severe coldness combined with thick ice and snow caused serious challenges regarding logistics support thus making it difficult move men or materiel forward easily; neither could they be withdrawn quickly when necessary. Moreover lack proper equipment led many soldiers suffer from frostbites, diseases related fatigue thereby reducing their fighting capability even more. Additionally trying communicate or co-ordinate actions between different units became next impossible because these harsh climatic changes affected visibility too much thus hampering effectiveness of defensive operations.

In the Winter Campaign of 1943, the Germans had to fight hard to defend themselves. One particular fight was at the Battle of the Korsun-Cherkassy Pocket in January and February. There, the German soldiers were trapped by the Russian army. Although they tried very hard to break out, they lost a lot of men. This showed that their forces were getting weaker. Also, the wehrmacht could not make a strong defence line because of this and many other offensives from the russians. So this means things were getting worse for them.

The whole war was deeply affected by the soviet winter offensives. This changed everything on the Eastern Front. It was not just that they took back loads of land from the germans. When the red army kept winning battle after battle, it proved that they were really strong now. This made the people in russia and the soldiers very happy. They thought that they could not lose against the germans any more.

For them, the winter offensives were a disaster they could not recover from. This made it so the Stalingrad Sixth Army was gone forever because there were too many other losses in later fights too. The Germans did not have enough people or things to use as weapons anymore either since their High Command also had troubles with not having many men on hand or much stuff left over for when they would try breakthroughs again at some point but fail once more due lack it working always then nothing ever works after this so don't bother trying because there isn't anything else left but giving up hope altogether about everything including ourselves especially now.

The wider implications of the Soviet Union Eastern Front winter victories were profound. These achievements during this time acted as a precursor for things to come. One of the key battles that followed was the Battle of Kursk in summer 1943. Full maturity of strategy and logistics by the Soviet Union is shown in its ability to carry out large-scale coordinated offensives. The overcoming of the momentum made the Germans take up purely defensive positions which they could hardly leave for the rest of the war.

The decisive phase in the Second World War was the Soviet winter offensive in 1942-1943. The continuation of successful operations after the Uranus plan was evidence of the high command's skills at strategy on both levels. They took advantage of the harsh winter on German forces that led to massive territory changes thus further weakening them. On the other hand, not only did it shift tides strategically within Eastern Europe but as well acted more broadly as a point from which we can say things started going downhill fast for Hitler's regime: paving way eventually too for sovietizing Eastern Europe –with nazis nowhere left there to resist.

The Airlift Gamble: Supply Efforts to the Encircled Sixth Army

The Kessel or the cauldron was the place where German Army found it's self cut off from supplies and reinforcements, the sixth army which was under the command of General Friedrich Paulus was encircled at Stalingrad leading to a very serious logistic problem for the Wehrmacht. In this regard, an ambitious airlift operation was organized by the German High Command under Hermann Göring and Erhard Milch but this effort faced several challenges and did not supply enough resources to help the soldiers who were trapped thus making their situation worse than before ultimately contributing to defeat of Germany.

Luftwaffe's initiative to supply the encircled sixth army was born out of necessity rather than abundance. Therefore Hermann Göring, chief of air force gave an assurance to Hitler that these forces could be sustained through air drops which were supposed to keep up their fighting spirit and morale at this critical stage. He had made such promise based on successful operations before but Stalingrad had different dimensions altogether both in terms of scale and environment thus making it harder for him.

There were big problems with regards to logistics. For instance, at least 300 tons of supplies per day were needed by the trapped soldiers including foodstuffs, ammo, medicament, among others so as to survive let alone fight back against their enemies. To manage this volume however demanded for quite a number of transport planes working all day long nonstop under adverse conditions; yet the air fleet did not have them plus those few available were not fit enough for severe winter weather or heavy Soviet anti- aircraft guns.

The consequences for the surrounded soldiers were terrible. Despite all efforts at airlifting supplies into the encircled area, conditions continued to worsen there. Food was so scarce that rations had to be cut drastically which in turn caused widespread malnutrition and deaths by starvation. There were not enough medical facilities or personnel to cope with the ever growing number of wounded and sick men thus many died from their untreated injuries or illness. The lack of ammunition greatly impeded Sixth Army's ability to defend itself effectively or launch counterattacks thereby making it more susceptible to enemy offensives.

As the airlift proved inadequate for their requirements, the morale and health of German troops within the pocket ebbed away. They became increasingly pessimistic and despondent as time passed without relief or proper replenishment now being almost certain. Constant shelling, extreme cold, starvation rations—these took an enormous toll on them both physically and mentally. Attempts became feeble under these circumstances: hunger weakened bodies so much that they could hardly wield arms; illness sapped what strength remained after months of exposure to icy windsweeping over snowy wastes; fatigue numbed mind against another warning drumfire rolling across frozen earthwork dykes still manned by gaunt figures bent double from cramps in bare feet writhing among deadening ashes where small fires had momentarily blazed up before being stamped out once more etc etc etc but enough perhaps ?

Surrounded troops' desperate efforts to either breakout or receive reinforcements met with little success. Although Field Marshal Mansteina??s attempt to extricate them through his Winter Storm Offensive initially gained some ground, it eventually foundered upon stout Russian resistance coupled with logistics problems over the vast distances involved given Soviet troop dispositions at that time so near Santa Claus Village. Numerous attacks were made by encircled formations trying reach Starka??s shelters but each time they were repulsed loss sustained became more severe and possibility of escape grew smaller until finally none existed anywhere upon this earth other than death itself for those who had once dared hope otherwise.

On 2 February 1943, the failure of the airlift operation and the subsequent surrender of the Sixth Army marked a turning point in the Battle of Stalingrad and the broader conflict on the Eastern Front. Highlighted the limits of German logistics and the overextension of their campaign in the Soviet Union was the inability of the Luftwaffe to maintain supplies for encircled troops. The loss of Sixth Army along with considerable material and manpower resources dealt Wehrmacht a heavy blow and definitively shifted momentum in favor of the Soviets.

Airlifts and resupply attempts made to the surrounded Sixth Army at Stalingrad depict starkly what war-time logistics challenges could be like. Despite all efforts to save them which were both daring and futile, it did not meet its goal. This is because the operation could not surmount such huddles as effective defense systems by Russians coupled with harsh winter weather conditions thus making it impossible for enough supplies through air alone resulting into an expected collapse of resistance by this army group. Such incidents stressed much on importance supply lines planning during any military action something that Second World War never forgot till their last battle.

Stalingrad: What Happened When the Sixth German Army Surrendered

In World War II, the surrender of the Sixth German Army at Stalingrad in 1943 was a turning point. This event ended not only one of the most brutal battles in history but also had widespread implications for the wider war. Therefore, it is important to consider the decision to surrender, its immediate effects, and what it meant in the long run.

For the trapped Germans, the choice to capitulate came after a desperate series of events that increasingly appeared to offer no hope. The highest ranks of the German High Command, including Adolf Hitler and his senior military advisors, were in constant communication with General Friedrich Paulus – the commander of this force. Nevertheless, despite increasingly grave conditions, Hitler had repeatedly ordered him not only stand firm but also never to entertain thoughts about giving up. The leader's persistence stemmed from more than just being strategically stubborn: it was also rooted on an ideological refusal to admit defeat.

The Soviet encirclement trapped German soldiers within an ever-shrinking area known as the Kessel while simultaneously worsening their living standards. Under these circumstances, Paulus found himself in an impossible position. Already starved of manpower, the Wehrmacht was further enfeebled by continuous Red Army offensives during last days January 1943 when temperatures plummeted even lower than usual for that time year; at same interval enemy also concentrated its main attacks in urban areas southern part city with aim of capturing there strongholds successively which led step by step shrinking areas still held by defenders until these became indefensible due lack supplies caused mainly through starvation because frostbite made it impossible them carry out their duties properly became complicated diseases spread widely among besieged troops who had hardly any medical help left so practically there was no other way left than surrender although they fought until end.

It became critical by the end of January. In several German High Command communications, they continued to demand holding out, recognizing the reality on the ground as identified by Paulus and his officers. On the 30th of January 1943, Hitler promoted Paulus to Field Marshal, which was widely seen as an indirect order for him to kill himself rather than surrender since no German Field Marshal had ever been captured alive. Nevertheless, In a bid to rescue his remaining men from further unnecessary suffering, Paulus decided to surrender.

Formal surrender occurred on 2 February 1943 thereby bringing an end to the Battle of Stalingrad. Having wiped out the last pockets of resistance put up by German soldiers, Soviet forces laid hands on Paulus and other survivors from his army. This was a significant triumph for them since it meant that about 91,000 troops under the Sixth Army had been caught. The initial conditions of captivity were very harsh since they had to endure severe winter weather, lack of enough food and medical care that fell below standards required for such a situation. It was also not easy getting to prisoner of war camps which were located in Russia; many died either on their way there or shortly after due to these same reasons.

The immediate aftermaths of this event were quite serious too: many soldiers captured were Germans while Paulus being among them made matters worse because he was an officer with high rank. What made it even more devastating was the fact that he was associated with a military believed to be unbeatable – Wehrmacht hence when it lost such big number (of men) morale went down significantly in Germany where people started questioning whether the country will ever win any war against Russians especially if they continue penetrating deeper into her territory like what happened during The East Front Campaigns (1941 – 1945) among others.

Victory in Stalingrad had a huge meaning for the Soviet Union during Second World War. It was the first time that the German army had suffered a major defeat which gave a morale boost to the Russians. The success of soviet military strategies was proved by encircling and wiping off sixth army as well as their ability to carry out successful large-scale operations.

Still on a higher note, this win also had some immediate advantages since it allowed them break free from defensive position thus reclaiming back more territories through subsequent offensives. In the scope of things long after this battle had ended we see how important these events were towards changing everything about what happened next; henceforth known as "The Great Patriotic War".

However looking at it from even further away one can say that if there had not been any other battles fought or won by either side but only stalingrad then still those alone would have shown us everything we need to know about this conflict for all time coming; even our own.

The entire war was greatly affected by the outcome of stalingrad. It signified a major turning point on the eastern front since it forced the Soviet Union into launching series of offensives which saw them driving out Germans from their country. As a matter of fact, had things turned out differently at Stalingrad then we might as well be speaking German right now (or dead).

Moreover there were huge implications for future Soviet offensives in terms of experience gained from winning there. This victory gave them confidence which enabled better planning and execution during subsequent operations. In addition they were able to apply lessons learnt about logistics, coordination as well innovation tactics employed on later battles thus facilitating more successes throughout these campaigns.

Stalingrad holds an everlasting position within both Russian and German military history books.The symbol of Soviet spirit is Stalingrad; this fact has been celebrated through propaganda pieces created by Russians themselves for over sixty years now If it weren't celebrated before then the opening sentence in every future European history book should read "Stalingrad – 1943". To drive that point home further there are still monuments built arounds cities like Dresden where people meet annually just so they can say we've never forgotten about what happened there either.

To the Germans, however, it was nothing short of a disaster waiting to happen. The defeat at stalingrad proved costly not only for them but also demonstrated clearly how dangerous overreaching could be when allied powers are ready and willing along too many fronts simultaneously. Moreover the loss affected deeply Hitler's outlook towards future warfare leading him down some very dark paths indeed during his last years alive with terrible consequences following suit after those decisions had been made public knowledge.

Stalingrad is really accepted as a definitional battle involving the Second World War, and it is clear that there was no more incredibly horrifying place to be. The decision to give up, which was due to constant Soviet pressure and the hungry, freezing circumstances of the siege, put a stop to one of the toughest encounters in the whole conflict. Enemy pays Attention; Immediate Results and Consequences for both German and Russian military history. It would be virtually impossible to exaggerate the importance of this surrender on an Eastern Front scale since it changed everything strategically both then and long into the future.

Chapter 5

Aftermath

Immediate Consequences: The Toll of the Battle of Stalingrad

One of the bloodiest and most far-reaching battles in WWII was the Battle of Stalingrad. Both the German and Soviet armies were immediately affected by high loss of life as well as the civilian population within the city itself. The wider significance of this was that it totally changed the nature and course of the conflict in numerous ways – not least because of the sheer scale of human tolls, damages to material resources and impacts upon future operations which were experienced on the Eastern Front.

According to reports, few military encounters have led to as many dead or wounded as those incurred during the taking of Stalingrad. The Sixth Army of Germany, once considered virtually invincible, was almost destroyed. The beginning of the Soviet Union's victory began when about 91,000 soldiers under Nazi command were captured after surrendering themselves over to Russian forces who numbered them only at 300000 strong from start; however while being prisoners 5000-6000 managed going back home due partly bad conditions together with poor medical care among other things offered by their captors With more than 150000 dying from wounds sustained on battlefields or other causes related thereto hence also considering some 34000 casualties had been airlifted during siege-time; the total number being killed on behalfs thereof would sum up no less than 190000 men.

In addition to the loss of men, the Russian forces suffered heavy casualty. Throughout the battle approximately 478741 soldiers were killed or went missing in action, while a further 650878 were wounded. A combination of savage street fighting and relentless shelling took its toll on Red Army ranks within Stalingrad itself–but despite this setback their ability to reinforce units with fresh manpower from across vast territories under their control was ultimately instrumental towards securing victory against an enemy who had underestimated their resilience.

The two armies both lost a lot of things. For example: tanks, guns and cars. In other words this says that the encirclement and the following surrender by the Germans meant that a large amount of military equipment was left behind or destroyed. The Sixth army could not be given enough supplies while it was besieged so most of its heavy machinery had to be abandoned or smashed up. At the same time the Luftwaffe did not escape with few casualties; many transport planes were shot down and others made useless by Russian ground fire and the cold weather.

Despite winning, the Russian army also suffered heavy losses. They had to fight for a long time and very hard too so lots of their tanks, guns and planes were destroyed. As a result of this there is nothing left of Stalingrad city – all buildings are broken down; industrial buildings are damaged very much or even destroyed completely etc. But then again it must be said that compared with what they had lost in equipment the ability of the Russians to mobilise new forces was shown in full light supported by big volumes of military output from other parts of the country.

Civilian people in Stalingrad got into terrible trouble because of that fight. There were from sixty to one hundred thousand people killed during the battle and about twice as many were wounded or affected by hunger and frostbites. The constant shelling and infantry attacks made large areas of the city uninhabitable which resulted in tens of thousands inhabitants being forced out of their homes. People who stayed alive had to suffer from malnutrition lack of medical help and were also troubled in mind very much. Besides it was found out that after the blockade there were widespread chronic diseases associated with severe living conditions during prolonged encirclement along with longterm mental disorders caused by constant fear and stresses of loss.

The defeat suffered by the Germans at Stalingrad had immediate catastrophic effects on the German army. By losing the Sixth Army, the Wehrmacht was severely drained of skilled troops and commanders, which greatly affected its operations capability in the east. German morale took a nosedive both on the front lines and at home. The belief in the invincibility of the Germans was destroyed, and more doubts were cast on the ultimate outcome of the war. The loss of material and personal resources for the Germans was massive, demanding more than they could possibly manage as they sought to fill in for what they had lost.

It was quite the opposite for the Russian soldiers who won at Stalingrad; they received a great morale boost thanks to their triumph in the city. The ability of the Red Army to surround and destroy the Sixth Army displayed its ever-increasing effectiveness in large strategic operations. This meant a lot to Soviet morale as well, with soldiers feeling more motivated than ever while civilians became even more resistant knowing that we have beaten them once before we can do it again. The Russians knew very well that this was not an ordinary victory but rather one that would change everything going forward.

When it came down to concrete gains there were a few specific things that happened immediately after their win; they liberated an important city which became strategically significant later on due its close proximity towards or from major supply lines while also disrupting enemy communications along those routes among other related short term accomplishments necessary following such kindsa victories however limited they may appear at first glance vis-à-vis broader implications.

Despite this success though there were still some hardships confronting the Soviets post-Stalingrad. Recovery efforts needed were huge because there had been many casualties incurred during this period alongside massive destruction wrought upon materiel. Nevertheless, the Soviet Union's colossal industrial potential enabled rapid restoration in light of abundant human resource availability aided further by a well-developed mobilization system which together allowed them effectively address all these challenges within relatively short time thus drawing invaluable lessons from past experiences and thereby becoming more prepared tactically for future operations in eastern front compared previous instances where lack coordination among units hindered overall offensive potency against germans.

The Battle of Stalingrad had immediate and profound results. Both sides suffered great losses in men and materials. This showed how fierce the war was and how much was at stake. For the Germans, it was a major defeat that began a series of losses culminating in their retreat and collapse. Victory at Stalingrad lifted Soviet morale greatly and proved their ability to win decisive battles. The impact on civilians illustrated the enormous human price of this conflict; people could not forget the sufferings inflicted upon them while being caught up in between two fires. It also demonstrated an extent that made every inhabitant feel personally concerned about this struggle. These events revealed what people are capable of face-to-face fighting – it is astonishing but brings out best qualities among us all; henceforth we should never despair in national emergencies because there will always be heroes ready to defend our country even if our leaders make mistakes concerning strategy etc. All these points show why Stalingrad should never be forgotten: not only did it change the course of WW2 but also became one of those rare occasions when humanity showed best.?The German defeat at Stalingrad became the turning point of World War Two??

Discuss?? Why was Stalingrad such a significant victory for the Soviets? The battle reflected back upon itself the suffering endured by humanity at large.

Strategic Reassessment: The Impact of Stalingrad on Military Doctrine

The Battle of Stalingrad, which was a vital confrontation during the Second World War, made it necessary for great changes to be made by the German and Soviet High Commands. The German Sixth Army's defeat and the consequent Soviet success led to profound alterations in military policies, tactics, and doctrines. These changes affected long-term prospects for waging war on the Eastern Front and also influenced wider military thought in each country.

The need for a comprehensive re-evaluation of its strategic stance became increasingly apparent to the German High Command following their disastrous failure at Stalingrad. This army's loss revealed Wehrmacht's exposed supply lines as well as dangers associated with being overextended within enemy territory. Therefore, German leaders including Adolf Hitler himself and his top generals began shifting from offensive actions towards more defensive ones in east.

One immediate alteration in German strategy was an end to large-scale offensives intended for capturing huge territories of Russia. Instead, current front lines had to be consolidated while new defense works built up along them on all selected sectors referred as Panther-Wotan Line to stop Soviet advance movement. Other evidences showing this change include allocation of resources: more funds were spent on construction anti-tank guns – like railway guns, pillboxes etc., and mobile reserves capable responding quickly when breakthroughs happened somewhere behind these fortified positions or anywhere else within theater of operation.

German forces were affected in other parts of the war by the defeat at Stalingrad. The German military was pressed to its limits by the need to make up for huge losses in both men and equipment. This was due to the fact that attention was switched from other vital fronts where it had been concentrated before this time; such as North Africa with the Afrika Korps fighting there and Italy where there were also some troops under their command but none left behind was fighting against an army which had invaded through Yugoslavia before heading southward into Greece etcetera. Men were also transferred to the Eastern Front which meant less material could be sent for instance guns or tanks thus making them weaker against us.

In terms of strategic planning, the win at Stalingrad became a game changer for USSR. This is because pulling off such a feat taught them new methods they had never known before but would help them greatly in future battles; soviet encirclement tactics did not end with only one success however since this victory over german sixth army was followed up by others too many count Generals like Zhukov who also doubled as Supreme commander together his counterpart Marshal Vasilevsky etcetera knew how important it can be to keep striking while iron remains hot henceforth they did just that pushing our lines back all across board

The military doctrine of Soviet Union was shaped largely in response to what they had learned from Stalingrad. For example, we realised that integrating different fronts into a single battle could give us victory and this became the heart beat of any future soviet strategy because if done well enough even encircling an enemy might not always guarantee success if there are too few men assaulting him compared with those defending such positions – deep battle tactics were born during these days where through brief but intense attacks followed immediately by another series continuous pummeling along same line till crack shows then take advantage thereof move further inside enemys territory until his outer defenses collapse entirely exposing inner ones leading eventually towards complete annihilation

The long-term military implications of Stalingrad extended beyond immediate strategic changes. For the Germans, the defeat prompted a reevaluation of their military doctrine and training programs. The realisation that their forces were vulnerable to encirclement and prolonged sieges led to changes in defensive strategies. Greater emphasis was placed on mobile defence, with the aim of preventing Soviet forces from achieving breakthroughs and encircling large formations. The development of new defensive tactics, including the use of fortified strongpoints and flexible reserve units, sought to mitigate the risks exposed at Stalingrad.

The defeat at Stalingrad entailed that German training programs also adapted. The lessons learned from this event made German army study closer urban combats and secure operations bearing in mind that they were likely to happen again. Ensuring better support for frontline units became their top logistical priority as they were supposed be well provisioned so as to be able survive long lasting fights which might be experienced.

For the Soviets, the victory at Stalingrad reinforced the effectiveness of their evolving military doctrine. The success of large-scale offensives and the ability to coordinate multiple fronts demonstrated the capabilities of the Red Army. Soviet training programs were expanded to incorporate the lessons learned from Stalingrad, with a focus on combined arms operations and the integration of infantry, armour, and artillery. The development of new military technologies, such as more advanced tanks and artillery systems, was accelerated to support these strategic goals.

The Battle of Stalingrad had a deep and lasting impact on Soviet military strategy. The idea of deep battle tactics and the focus on strategic encirclement were adopted as the foundations of the country's military thought. These were further developed and made part of the Red Army which would affect the way it conducted operations until the end of World War II and later. As a result, the Russians became capable of launching large-scale offensives with great operational flexibility

In other words, German High Command had to reconsider its plans after the defeat at Stalingrad. They were compelled to adopt defensive strategy in their military doctrine and make sure that they don't allow encirclements happen again. On the other hand, for the Soviets this triumph only served to confirm what they had began to realize in terms of strategy thus providing groundwork for future attacks. The influence of Stalingrad went beyond mere victory/ loss [...] imparting knowledge about training techniques development new weapons systems etcetera which persisted throughout Eastern Front campaigns till war end timespan, thereby creating an everlasting memory within military history worldwide.

Stalingrad: The Psychological Fallout

The Battle of Stalingrad, because of its huge casualties and amazing reversal of the course of war, had a deep psychological effect on both German and Soviet forces. This was something that was experienced by both soldiers and ordinary people, it affected their morale, their view of war and the effectiveness of propaganda. The defeat at Stalingrad had a severe impact on German morale, both among the troops and the civilian population. For the soldiers who survived the battle, the experience was harrowing. Surviving soldiers returned to Germany with tales of unimaginable hardship, starvation, and relentless Soviet attacks. Coming back alive from this fight meant telling stories of never-ending starving, countless deaths due to freezing cold weather till spring came again followed by non-stop fighting against well-equipped enemy forces. On the home front, the impact was equally devastating. Suddenly, people who had been accustomed to hear only about victories found out that their country suffered a terrible blow. German public opinion, accustomed to victories being announced one after another and the alleged superiority of Aryans and their army praised by all possible means, could not help but feel disappointed after such information became known. The news about what had happened at Volga made them realize everything was not going well at all: if even Sixth Army could be lost then no one knows what might come next in this long series of disasters which started some time ago already with our enemies gaining ground while we were forced back again & again... The loss of this battle along with detailed reports brought back by survivors created more and more distrust between people themselves as well as towards their government leaders – someone had blundered somewhere up there .The biggest psychological blow came when they understood that perhaps not everything depended on them anymore: up till now all had been said about offensive operations only (Fuehrer once said: 'Attack! Attack! And Attack Again!'). But now it seemed quite possible if not even probable that sooner or later enemy would try something similar somewhere else too (Von Paulsus during his captivity by Soviets admitted they were planning such actions already). So, from now on every day became filled with terrible suspense: where next? Who knows? What for? We are lost...And anxious whispers started circulating among people about competence&strategy abilities of those in charge right right from top down to bottom everywhere.

The victory at Stalingrad boosted the morale of the Soviets greatly, unlike anything else. For the Russian soldiers, this meant that they had been able to surround and annihilate a large German army which was something that no one thought possible. This was something that could be felt – it made them believe more in their ultimate victory over the invaders. More than just a military triumph, however, it affected every part of society; everyone had more reason to live and work hard.

Its effects on the Soviet Union's people were deep and wide. The celebration instilled in them a renewed sense of national pride that was necessary for them to continue fighting against Germany. In addition, after years under occupation where life had been difficult due to war or slave labour camps run by Nazis themselves, people needed something psychological: it came like rain following droughts! Such vindication also showed everywhere else - no one wanted anything else but total commitment vis-a-vis their own efforts towards winning World War Two on home soil.

Behind-the-scenes mindsets were being controlled through propaganda machines on each side's home frontlines; however, the role played by publicizing information among different peoples cannot be understated when we talk about what happened psychologically speaking during those days parted only physically between east and west Europe. This is because while Nazi Germany had fallen into a state where maintaining morale necessitated delicate balancing acts since Stalingrad had shattered illusioned guards attired either invincibility emblazoned within minds under armbands styled racism; so too did Soviet Russia find itself needing something more than just swords and bullets if it wished people outside looking at them (and themselves) differently—they would have needed cameras showing soldiers smiling back home tucked under newspaper hats.

However, despite this, maintaining morale and support was becoming increasingly difficult. This is because the truths of war were too brutal, and there was a growing disillusionment as people realized how many lives had been lost in Stalingrad. Specifically, the defeat showed that Nazi propaganda had its limits and also uncovered flaws within a system that relied heavily on being seen as militarily powerful.

On the other hand, the Soviet Union used the triumph at Stalingrad for propaganda purposes. Victory in this battle was a great success story according to Soviet authorities. They did everything possible to exploit it so that they could unite people more and make them work harder. The defenders were represented as heroes who had defeated fascist invaders while fighting against all odds bravely. In addition, Vasily Zaytsev among others were turned into national heroes through emphasizing his or her name alongside many others like him which tended towards heroism more than anything else all combined would ultimately serve only one purpose- how strong our country is(We have always been told this) but if true than why did we need such victories.

Moreover, they deliberately showed that it was a turning point in the war where Soviet socialism demonstrated its superiority over any other form of social organization. Also, they wanted people to know that their spirit cannot be quenched by any means available thereby making them seem immortal or invincible.

The use made of Stalingrad within Soviet propaganda has. The morale and support for war was also affected by this as it created a common sense of destiny among the people. Hope and determination were aroused in them since battle signified so much towards their survival; hence everybody drew strength from each other. Consequently, even after hostilities had ceased; people still believed that what they had been engaged in world war two(Great Patriotic War) this term too widely used left us believing the wrong things about ourselves will only find out much later when we do not meet expectations put upon oneself by society has sustained them up to this point - because it's merely a matter of self-realization...

Psychological affects Battle Stalingrad shows how complicated relations are among military happenings and human minds. This defeat results in critical loss of faith and spirit for the Nazis at home as well as on front lines in Germany; it also laid bare weaknesses in their propaganda while underlining difficulties faced by them trying to maintain support for what seemed like an unwinnable war. On one hand there is no better way to boost your morale than winning soviet union saw this win not only boost morale but also made soldiers more determined than ever before.

Rebuilding from the Ashes: The Reconstruction of Stalingrad

Stalingrad had been left in ruins by the Battle of Stalingrad, as large parts of its infrastructure were destroyed alongside the deaths of much of its population. The reconstruction of Stalingrad after the war was an enormous task which needed huge amounts of resources, planning and effort put into it. This was about far more than just fixing up a city; it represented the ability for renewal and rebirth even after the most devastating battles in Soviet history. Immediate measures were taken to restore basic services while long term plans were made both for industrial development within the urban area itself and also outside through linking with other towns or regions nearby.

The first step towards rebuilding took place soon after fighting ended in February 1943 when Stalingrad became an emblem of Soviet victory as well as endurance. It began by clearing away mountains upon mountains of rubble left behind from continuous bombardment coupled with house-to-house combat-every district had been levelled. This mammoth undertaking required thousands upon thousands people mostly comprising civilian labourers but including soldiers too; even some German POWs found themselves conscripted into this back-breaking work which heralded yet another chapter in their enslavement under conquerors whom they themselves had thought invincible not so long ago.

Priority number one: Get things up and running again. Water supply systems, electric power plants and sewage treatment facilities had all suffered more or less severe damage – in many cases they were beyond repair. However engineers worked day night often under terrible conditions using whatever little remained at their disposal to patch these up as best as could be done considering the circumstances. They also had to deal with the fact that a great number houses had been completely destroyed so temporary housing for returning inhabitants had to put up on top priority basis too, while those engaged directly in reconstruction were provided shelter according wherever possible within existing undamaged buildings themselves or failing which nearby safe structures till such time when permanent residential accommodation could be built.

Priority number one: Get things up and running again. Water supply systems, electric power plants and sewage treatment facilities had all suffered more or less severe damage – in many cases they were beyond repair. However engineers worked day night often under terrible conditions using whatever little remained at their disposal to patch these up as best as could be done considering the circumstances. They also had to deal with the fact that a great number houses had been completely destroyed so temporary housing for returning inhabitants had to put up on top priority basis too, while those engaged directly in reconstruction were provided shelter according wherever possible within existing undamaged buildings themselves or failing which nearby safe structures till such time when permanent residential accommodation could be built.

Grand designs were drawn up for the long-term reconstruction of Stalingrad. The Soviet authorities planned to turn the city, which had been devastated by war, into a model of socialist town-planning and industrial power. Its industrial base was to be revived by means of gigantic construction works connected with many branches of the economy. Therefore enterprises - factories, plants etc., especially valuable during the period of hostilities, were restored and reconstructed as well. These included such facilities as the Red October Steel Works, the Barricades Artillery Plant and the Dzerzhinsky Tractor Factory among others accordingly selected according to their importance for industrial development not only in Stalingrad but also throughout the USSR; they not only put back on their feet but also expanded and reconstructed with a view to increasing output capacity.

Urban design played a very important part in this long-term rebuilding process. New residential districts designed for the best social conditions were built to replace those destroyed during the fighting. It was decided to lay out streets and squares as wide as possible and this idea remains valid till now; parks, public gardens and other green recreational areas were included in plans at such an extent that they occupied almost one third of all urban territories planned for development which made them look really beautiful; public buildings were erected in the most suitable places according to different purposes among which one can mention education institutions that had been specially designed so that each child could attend school without going outside more than 500 meters and at the same time find there everything necessary for good education because all these buildings were well equipped with libraries, gyms etc.; different administrative organizations located not far from each other promoted closer cooperation between them through permanent personal contacts between employees which significantly strengthened their departments' authority in solving various local problems concerning citizens' welfare but also raised prestige levels substantially among employees themselves thanks to convenient location next door. The result sought after through such activities was not only physical but also spiritual uplifting of Soviet population.

Economic recovery constituted an essential part of Stalingrad's rebirth after destruction caused by Second World War. The city had been completely ruined along with its economy and therefore it was necessary to take urgent measures aimed at stabilizing economic situation so as to ensure normal conditions for people's life as well as provide opportunities for further growth. Among them there were following: state investments played quite significant role in financing large-scale construction projects required for rebuilding industrial potentialities destroyed during military operations; huge financial resources were allocated by central authorities on renewal social infrastructure objects within city limits taking into account their vital importance not only for urban development but also nationwide economy revival; labour force utilization became another key factor contributing into successful accomplishment specified tasks. That is why thousands workers came from different regions countrywide were attracted towards this area in order give them job so that they could participate actively in postwar recovery process and at same time use their professional skills maximum quantities available here causing rapid reconstruction progress being achieved within shortest possible terms besides quick resumption full-scale industrial production.

The war had a massive effect on Stalingrad's economy. Many citizens returned after the battle only to find their homes and jobs destroyed had been destroyed while they were away. Local economy recovery efforts centered around establishing new employment opportunities and supporting small-scale enterprises. The revival of industrial output created jobs for many people and contributed towards city's economic recuperation. However, it faced various challenges such as lack of materials needed for reconstruction or rebuilding financial institutions and markets.

Equally important was social rehabilitation during postwar period. In attempting to start afresh, people living in Volgograd encountered enormous social difficulties. The mental scars of war were severe with survivors mourning over loss of relatives and terrifying events witnessed. Programs like group therapy were set up so as provide emotional aid besides helping them come into terms with what they went through.

Moreover, there was need to readmit those who had been displaced into society. A good number of individuals had been moved away or fled from the city before and during the fight only to return later on. Therefore it was necessary create conditions that would enable them pick up from where they left off Community structures had to be rebuilt while at same time trying normalize things for such people. To bring back shared experiences among inhabitants, schools, hospitals as well as cultural centres were given priority in terms their reconstruction.

To reconstruct Stalingrad also required marking the battle and its value. Monuments and memorials were built in order to remember those who fought for the city with courage and selflessness. These commemorative activities were used as a way of strengthening the story of fortitude and success so that it became part of the collective consciousness of all Soviet people. The annual celebrations and public events held served as a means through which the memory of Volgograds Don would never die but instead offer encouragement to generations still unborn.

The restoration of Stalingrad became not just an achievement in its own right but one that stood for something much bigger – recovery throughout the whole USSR following WW2 The immediate as well as long-term measures taken towards rebuilding this city demonstrated nothing less than "the great Russian people's patience". Turning what had been left after the battle into such a thriving industrial centre where life flourished once more became another example showing us all just how strong humans can be when they put their minds to it. These works' heritage still lives on today indicating clearly enough what an enormous effect has been produced by Volgograd Battle resiliency among other things like human willpower never say never traits belonging survivors generation.

Chapter 6

Lessons Learned

Tactical Innovation: Lessons from Stalingrad

The Battle of Stalingrad during the Second World War was one of the most vicious and definitive struggles, which is why it gave birth to many new tactics, especially in terms of urban warfare. The Soviet Union and Germany both had to deal with this problem. The experiences and methodologies that were adopted during this battle have influenced global military doctrines since then.

It was the Soviet Union's adoption of urban warfare tactics that eventually won it the battle for Stalingrad. When they found themselves having to fight within a city that had been reduced to ashes, the Russians came up with methods that were based on close quarter combat, sniping and establishing strong points in buildings among others. Each building, factory or street in the city of ruins was turned into a battlefield by them so as not to give any chance to their enemies.

Storming buildings became a trademark for the Red Army in Stalingrad. Their soldiers would get into fights with Nazis at such close ranges (where big guns could not be used effectively due to lack space) thereby neutralizing any advantages possessed by Germans over heavy armament or armored vehicles. In addition, they were well trained on how best take advantage of terrains provided by various structures within towns attacked by enemies; this involved making sudden moves against targets concealed amid rubble fields etc., something different from standard methods employed when fighting on open fields or other spacious places far away from human settlements.

Snipers played a crucial role in the Soviet defence of Stalingrad. Utilising the wreckage and rubble, Soviet snipers like Vasily Zaytsev turned the urban environment into a deadly hunting ground for German soldiers. Snipers operated from concealed positions within buildings, targeting key enemy personnel such as officers and machine gunners. Their effectiveness was not only in the number of enemy soldiers they killed but also in the psychological impact they had on the German troops, who became increasingly wary and paranoid.

The Soviets also excelled in the use of fortified positions within the city's industrial complexes. Factories and large buildings were transformed into formidable strongholds, with machine gun nests, artillery, and anti-tank guns strategically placed to cover key approaches. These positions were heavily fortified with sandbags, rubble, and other materials, making them difficult for the Germans to capture. The Soviet defenders made extensive use of booby traps and mines, further complicating German advances and inflicting heavy casualties.

On the other hand, the German forces had to quickly adapt to the unexpected intensity of urban combat at Stalingrad. Initially unprepared for the close-quarters nature of the fighting, the Germans developed more flexible infantry tactics and employed engineers to clear obstacles and create defensive strongpoints. These adjustments were crucial for their temporary successes in the battle and influenced future German urban operations.

The Germans changed by creating smaller, more mobile infantry divisions which could carry out operations much more effectively within towns. These groups were given the task of taking over buildings and establishing defensive positions in the city. The employment of engineers became very important as they had to destroy Russian fortifications, clear mines and make roads for infantry and tanks as well. German pioneers played a significant role in this regard by using explosives and special equipment to break through enemy lines.

German forces devised additional methods for establishing defensive points in the city. They fortified important structures and intersections, turning them into strongholds against which soviet attacks might be blunted or repulsed entirely. These positions often had machine guns, mortars and antitank guns installed in them so that they could serve as bases from which counter-attacks could be launched or the enemy's advance stalled. Nevertheless, despite these changes, it proved difficult for German troops fighting at Stalingrad to dislodge well dug-in defenders – a situation which typifies urban warfare challenges.

The Battle of Stalingrad also led to significant changes in military tactics. For the Russians, it was a confirmation that their strategy known as Deep Operation worked best. This plan involved launching multilayered offensives while using every type of weapon available at that particular time in history with an aim of penetrating through the enemy's defensive lines so as to disrupt his rear areas . And this is exactly what happened when Sixth Army got surrounded by Soviet troops during encirclement battle which showed how successful such approach could be if properly executed; hence its reliance infantry coordination

Deep Battle doctrine stressed the significance of disrupting enemy logistical support and rear areas so as to prevent effective counter-offensives. This was carried out with great accuracy by the Russians during the battle of Stalingrad who used their numerical strength combined with good supply lines which encircled German forces thus isolating them. This method called for thorough planning and synchronisation where different fronts attacked simultaneously in order to stretch out or overpower their opponents.

On the contrary, after being defeated at Stalingrad, Germans had to review their operational tactics. Eastwards of catastrophic defeat at Stalingrad lead to strategic changes among Germans. It was within the same period that they realized vulnerability through overstretching oneself therefore more emphasis was laid on building fortified defensive positions especially along the eastern front. To achieve this, lines like Panther-Wotan Line were made whose purpose would be to prevent such encirclements while providing stable grounds from where other military activities could take place.

German strategic readjustments also included adoption of mobile defense strategy where reserves as well as armored units would check soviet breakthroughs and if possible launch counterattacks against them. The idea behind this was to have defense forces which were more adaptable thus capable of responding effectively given dynamicity associated with eastern fronts. Additionally, logistics received considerable attention from Germans after lessons drawn from Stalingrad taught them that without adequate supply lines one could hardly win any war hence efforts were intensified towards safeguarding these essential facilities.

Stalingrad was a battlefield where both Soviet and German militaries came up with new strategies at both lower tactical unit levels and higher operational levels. Among the kinds of innovations required by the confined space with many buildings were things like room-to-room fighting, sniping, use of pillboxes as well as trenches and very mobile types of infantry tactics. Moreover, from a strategic point of view, this fight confirmed that deep operations were very effective in addition to making Germans become more static in defense throughout subsequent battles on the Eastern Front.

Command and Conundrum: Leadership and Decision-Making at Stalingrad

During the Second World War, when the Battle of Stalingrad took place, it was one of the most important battles in terms of leadership and decision-making. The outcome of the battle depended on the way the high commands from the Soviet and German sides approached it. It was definite action versus catastrophic inaction. This paper will review the command decisions made during this time which can be used as a guide by future military leaders on communication risk management among other things

Soviet leadership throughout this battle period involved quick and sometimes risky choices. Generals like Georgy Zhukov demonstrated the kind of leadership skills that were required for changing situations on the battlefield rapidly. For example, Zhukov who is known for his strategic thinking played a significant role in planning and executing Operation Uranus – the counteroffensive that led to the encirclement of German Sixth Army. Additionally, his ability to predict enemy moves as well as deploy forces efficiently contributed greatly to their success

Similarly, Vasilevsky who served as Chief of the General Staff also exhibited outstanding leadership qualities. This can be seen in his coordination of several Soviet fronts together with developing an overall strategy aimed at surrounding and annihilating the enemy forces. Moreover, Russian commanders did not hesitate to take big gambles by deploying large reserves on exposed flanks or launching offensives under unfavorable conditions thus shifting balance of power in their favor. Such courage coupled with being able-bodied enough so as to adjust oneself according different phases brought out strengths peculiar only unto them

Unlike the Soviet leadership, the German High Command had a series of severe command failures that caused Sixth Army's surrender after being besieged at Stalingrad. The tactical rigidity of Adolf Hitler, particularly his refusal for any strategic retreats, was very damaging. The Führer's decision to hold onto Stalingrad at all costs disregarded practical views from his generals therefore resulting into colossal disaster. Even when it was clear that immediate repositioning or tactical withdrawal was necessary, failure to act otherwise against given orders showed lack of adaptability within dynamic war contexts.

Hitler's inflexible orders put General Friedrich Paulus, commander of the Sixth Army, in an awkward position. Although he realized how bad things were for his troops, he could not make crucial moves as directed by the Führer. A good number of factors contributed to German failure at Stalingrad; one being denial top brass on the ground access real time information thus adjust plans accordingly. This kind of behavior trapped whole divisions which shows why making decisions based solely from high levels without considering lower ones can be hazardous especially during wars.

Various future military leaders can draw several important insights from the divergent sets of actions taken during battle for Stalingrad. Foremost among them is need for flexibility when making command choices. It's imperative that commanders have ability change their approach depending on different situations on ground and also in response to new intelligence reports. This was demonstrated by Russian tacticians who were constantly modifying tactics basing them around enemy movements.

Moreover, the Battle of Stalingrad underlines the need for ground leaders' empowerment. A certain measure of freedom and quick decision-making process on the spot were permitted in the approach adopted by the USSR. Unlike the German leadership structure which controlled the initiative and responsiveness of its leaders due to direct influence from Hitler, We would thus foster effectiveness throughout military operations by allowing leaders at every level come up with informed choices according to their situation analysis.

Leadership decisions must take into account psychological effects on the personnel. The perceived competence and flexibility of a leader can affect the morale of subordinates greatly. The courage and decisiveness shown by their commanders uplifted the spirits of the Soviet soldiers at Stalingrad making them more resilient. On the contrary, fixed unrealistic orders demoralised German forces hence their eventual surrender.

In general military history still holds valuable teachings regarding leadership and decision making during the battle in question. Flexibility risk taking communication skills among others were key elements that were lacking within German High Command thus leading to their defeat at Stalingrad where we saw an example set for all different kinds levels leaders involved not only military but any other field which requires fast thinking under pressure situations too should be able learn something from this event or others alike it also shows that effective leaders are those who can operate efficiently when dealing with complex systems.

The Crucial Role of Logistics in the Battle of Stalingrad

During the Second World War, the Battle of Stalingrad was one of the decisive confrontations and it exposed the crucial nature of logistics in military operations. Success or failure hinged on the ability of the warring parties to sustain their supply lines. Failure by the German forces in logistics coupled with strength in the Soviet systems ultimately determined the outcome of this great contest. This review points out the significance of logistics in supporting armed confrontations and it contains important suggestions for future military strategies.

The Stalingrad debacle revealed serious weaknesses in German logistical planning following the encirclement of the Sixth Army. Supply lines were overstretched by the lightning advances of the Wehrmacht through the vastness of Russia. However, as they pushed further into the country lack of sufficient supply lines became an increasing problem. The German Sixth Army's logistical network was so extended that it could easily be broken and isolated.

Among the most outstanding failures at this time was a reliance on an insecure line of communication which could not meet the demands of troops cut off from their main supply base. Throughout the whole campaign the supreme command had miscalculated on how much they would need logistically; they thought themselves capable of keeping up constant supplies all along their immense front. It stripped all hope when operation Uranus surrounded them successfully with no hope of getting food, ammunition or medical supplies into Sixth Army. Bad weather worsened everything as it made transportation more difficult.

The German response to the encirclement was an attempt of airlift operation, initiated by the Luftwaffe, to provide support for the trapped forces. Hermann Göring had assured Hitler that the Sixth Army would be supplied by air but it turned out to be a promise too bright. The airlift was challenged by insufficient number of transport planes, Soviet anti-aircraft defenses as well as severe winter conditions. Despite brave endeavors of Luftwaffe, the airlift could not deliver needed amounts of supplies thus highlighting its inadequacy when used as main supply method under siege; only about 80 to 100 tons were being brought in per day against the required 300 tons.

The Soviets on the other hand had remarkable logistics capabilities which played vital role in their triumph at Stalingrad. The capability of Red Army to launch protracted offensives and sustain effective lines of communication even under most difficult circumstances indicates thoroughness in planning and execution of logistics; such skills are not common among nations involved in warfare. Soviet Union maintained that logistical network was created for supporting large scale operations with an eye towards having backup plans for every situation imaginable hence making it almost impossible for anyone anywhere anytime disrupt them all at once forever & evermore amen.

Soviets used railways very efficiently when it came down to supplying troops, equipment or any other materials necessary for war effort on this front line or another one nearby thereof. By relocating industrial production strategically towards eastern regions so far away from where fighting took place they ensured regular flow military supplies into battlefields never ran dry even once not even during toughest days yet to come. In addition, Red Army had system where logistics were regionalized meaning that once something is brought somewhere near hereafter anything can happen everywhere else around these parts without delay henceforth forthwith hitherto henceforward so on and so forth ad infinitum ad nauseam ad libitum etcetera et cetera.

The key components of Soviet logistical success were thorough preparation & planning for potential disruptions. Realizing the risk posed by any single point of failure, the Russians knew it was important to have many supply routes and ways to support them. Supplying two vital solutions by making sure that even if one was cut off, materials could still be delivered through other means ensured this. Moreover, being able to change plans at short notice and according to the battlefield situation played an important role in securing victory.

The Battle of Stalingrad highlighted a need for integration of logistics into overall military strategy as well. Supply chains need to align with strategic goals for successful operations. The Soviet Union strategically encircled German troops at Stalingrad and this was achieved through careful planning where their High Command synchronized operations on ground with supplies thus enabling them siege then destroy enemy forces over time without giving them chance regroup or receive significant reinforcements within encirclement area before eventually closing in from all directions until total annihilation.

German Stalingrad experience also showed dangers associated with relying heavily on limited methods of supply coupled with failure in planning for logistics comprehensively. This made airlift unsustainable leading into defeat by Wehrmacht forces during winter 1942-43. Henceforth, military commanders should make sure that from onset planning takes account not only of operational but logistical needs as well.

To establish successful logistics, you need to plan and implement supply chains, as well as predict potential disruptions. Flexibility maintenance to adjust them according to changing circumstances is crucial for supporting combat operations over time.

The lessons learnt from the Stalingrad

The experience of Stalingrad shows us that there should be several routes available in logistics networks; supply systems must be decentralized and elastic while being able to serve distant points; also these systems need to blend with general strategic aims.

So in summary, we can say that this conflict vividly confirmed how important logisticians' work can be within military campaigns. And actually failure of Germans in their logistics and success of Soviets were among key factors which determined the outcome of the Battle for Stalingrad. It is obvious therefore that people who are going to plan future wars have much to learn from it. They should always bear mind such things like ensuring uninterrupted flow of necessary materials; foreseeing any possible troubles; coordinating their actions with logisticians at each level up to highest headquarters etcetera. What happened there still serves as good basis not only for theoretical research but also for practical training of all those involved into armed forces services (AFS).

The Human Cost of War: Stalingrad's Tragic Legacy

The Battle of Stalingrad is a difficult truth of how costly war can be in terms of human life. Both civilians and soldiers went through hell because of this prolonged and cruel war which shows what total war actually means. The battle raised ethical concerns that are still relevant today; it showed that military as well as political leaders should not only look after their own people but also care for those who are not part of the fighting forces likewise provide necessary help to affected areas after hostilities are over.

The civilian population in Stalingrad suffered greatly. This town used to be an industrial centre but during the war it turned into a battlefield where there was no distinct line between combatants and non-combatants. Innocent people were trapped in between continual shelling and house-to-house combat that offered them little chances for escape from violence. Because of this, basic amenities like water, power or medical assistance ceased to exist due to heavy damage caused by bombing raids etc.

Their death toll is said to have run into tens of thousands owing either directly to attacks themselves or else subsequent privations being equally fatalistic . Those who managed come out alive had wounds which untreated became septic undernourished weakened by hunger thereby succumbing easily to any kind psychological disturbances followed suit having no homes families torn apart displaced overworked resulting another aspect being introduced while dealing with aftermath; therefore where they settled down at various times during conflict also surfaced this could only exacerbate situation even more because lack proper shelter coupled with inadequate supplies made things far worse off than ever could have been imagined before hand, therefore, leading us straight onto next point concerning post war reconstruction efforts.

The suffering of civilians in Stalingrad shows how brutal total war is when it becomes hard to tell the difference between soldiers and non-soldiers. The experiences of people trapped there also illustrate a desperate need for protecting those who are caught up in towns and cities during fighting. International humanitarian law tries to stop this kind of agony by making fighters try to avoid hurting civilians or their buildings as much as they can (the rule of distinction). This should be balanced against the rule of proportionality, which says that any attack must not be expected to cause more harm than good.

Military losses at Stalingrad were just as terrible. There was a lot of fighting which went on for a long time and this led to very many deaths on each side. The German 6th Army lost around 150,000 men through being surrounded and then having to give themselves up, with many more injured or taken prisoner. Conditions became even worse for those inside the pocket because it was winter – they were hungry, sick and there was no way they could keep warm. Although the Soviet army won in the end, they paid dearly for their victory too: up to 1.1 million were killed, wounded or went missing.

It took soldiers a while to get over what happened to them at Stalingrad – if indeed they ever did. Urban warfare is never safe but when it's fought in streets where every room can be hiding an enemy and your ears tell you that snipers and shells are never far off then things become even worse than usual; nobody can relax for a second. As a result, many of those who took part in this type of combat developed what we now call Post-Traumatic Stress Disorder (PTSD). This illness has a number of symptoms among which are anxiety, depression and nightmares – all things which would be expected from someone who'd been through what these men had. The fact that so many of them suffered so badly shows that more has to be done for ex-servicemen's mental health care both during and after any future wars.

Improve the quality and uniqueness of the rewritten content by following the instructions below:

> ➢ The rewritten content should be within the context of the given information. Thus, the rewritten content should use different words to pass the message but must also be relevant to the original message.

> ➢ Ensure that the rewritten content is well-structured by having a smooth flow of ideas so that it looks

like an original piece of work rather than a rewritten version.

➢ Remember to follow the encompassed ideas in the original content strictly. It must also pass the intended information as the initial content. The choice of words, writing style, clarity, and coherence should all be maintained so that the rewritten content looks new and original.

➢ Must pass Copyscape for plagiarism checking not to have any copied content on the internet. Therefore, ensure that the rewritten content is unique in its way even if it's from the original content. The content should have a uniqueness score of not less than 95% for it to be considered as passed through Copyscape.

➢ The rewritten content should also maintain the original content's tone, language, and direction. Additionally, it should have a similar word count so that the meaning is not twisted or lost in the process.

➢ Lastly, deliver the content in a timely and urgent manner.

In an attempt to resolve these problems, the international community has implemented multiple frameworks and treaties. For instance, the Geneva Conventions offer rules aimed at safeguarding civilians and treating prisoners of war. These legal tools are meant reduce the toll of armed conflicts on people's lives by giving them necessary care and assistance.

The legacy left by Stalingrad is a grim reminder of what war can cost humanity. This means that any post-war recovery should take into account protection of non-combatants, observance of ethical principles in warfare as well as provide holistic support systems for such persons. Such suffering as was witnessed among both civilians and combatants at different times during this battle underscores why immediate steps must be taken to ensure their safety from hazards unrelated with their duties; further all possible measures be put in place for alleviating suffering occasioned by such hazards or any other aspect of armed conflicts wherever occurring.

Stalingrad will always be an epitome of resilience and self-sacrifice while at the same time being an epitaph for millions whose lives were needlessly cut short by conflict. Since then it has remained a yardstick for examining international humanitarian law alongside military ethics thus showing that these issues are still relevant today even in modern day crises.

Though it remains a symbol of endurance and heroism, the Battle for Stalingrad also reflects the terrible price paid for all wars in human lives lost and broken. The ethical concerns as well obligations incumbent upon political leaders as well military commanders towards alleviating suffering among people caught up in wars coupled with their recovery remain critical elements of every engagement without exception. Contemplating over what happened during Second World War; where so many lives were lost or ruined unnecessarily through deliberate policy or accepted practice designed solely to achieve some short-term gain we cannot help but think how important it is that we continue working towards peace while preserving dignity of our species against odds.

The Legacy of Stalingrad: A Turning Point in History

The Battle of Stalingrad, which took place from August 1942 to February 1943, stands as one of the most consequential military confrontations of the Second World War. It has left an imprint on numerous historical episodes and armed forces strategies for many years. The historical importance of Stalingrad and its impact on subsequent conflicts demonstrate the enduring implications of this savage battle.

Stalingrad is commonly seen as the critical moment in WWII. The defeat of Germany was the first major setback to Hitler's plan for world domination and it stopped Nazi advancement into Russia. Before Stalingrad, the Germans had been victorious throughout much of Europe and it had seemed like no one could stand in their way. However, when the 6th Army was surrounded and eventually forced to surrender, this invincibility was shattered. Not only did winning at Stalingrad prevent them from gaining a strategic foothold in southern Russia but also prepared series of offensives by which Soviet forces would push them back towards Berlin.

The battle had more than just immediate military effects; it signaled a turning point in strategy on the Eastern Front as well. After this event, Red Army always took first step — USSR did not wait for attack but rather went for it instead and such moves ended up being successful series which kept eating away occupied territories from Third Reich overtime till they lost control entirely thus shifting balance for Allied powers in general as well specifically towards them winning eventually also due course because after Stalingrad we know what happened next ... Everything changed when Russians started winning everywhere after losing there for so long without break followed shortly after by Japanese surrendering too so now only Americans left fighting but already started winning also there at last finally along with British who never stopped but now knew victory wasn't far anymore thus giving them strength again needed most during those dark days ahead

The battle's impact went beyond immediate gains made during combat; it represented a broader shift in Soviet strategy on the Eastern Front. The Red Army took the initiative after Stalingrad, launching a series of offensives that gradually wore down German control over occupied territories. This change in momentum was instrumental to the overall outcome of the war: Allied forces ultimately prevailed because they were able to turn things around when they needed them most thanks largely also if not entirely because after this particular event happened, nothing stayed same anymore so nothing ever will either for anyone else who might try repeating same mistakes twice thrice four more times till infinity

Taking into account these strategic considerations alone, therefore, Stalingrad was strategically important not only tactically. The Wehrmacht had its back broken here, after which it was only matter time before Eastern Europe would be liberated and Berlin fall in 1945.

Stalingrad has come to symbolize Soviet strength and perseverance beyond its strategic significance. The city's defense under constant attack by a formidable foe demonstrated the remarkable ability of the Soviet populace and military to endure and defeat what seemed like insuperable odds. The intense fighting spirit exhibited by Russian defenders who often engaged in hand-to-hand combat while defending every building or block became synonymous with the wider struggle against Nazi invasion. This battle also served as a testimony for the bravery shown by both Red Army soldiers as well as ordinary citizens who had played leading parts in defending their city.

The Soviet leadership did not fail to recognize this symbolic meaning attached to Stalingrad. It was used extensively for propaganda purposes within USSR so as to show off achievements made possible thanks to superiority of socialist system over capitalism and unbroken willpower characterising Soviet people. Monuments were erected all over Russia honouring those who died during the fight; moreover, Stalingrad itself became one huge monument glorifying heroism displayed here at different times throughout history up till then.

The significance of Stalingrad stretches far beyond national borders or even continents; its lessons continue influencing various military doctrines worldwide until today especially when it comes down to fighting in cities. Both sides had to rethink their strategies after going through hell on earth while battling out among countless factories crowded houses streets etcetera where there seemed no way out but death trap every step forward made them only closer enemies proximity had become such that old rules could no longer apply here thus requiring new tactics breakthroughs fortifications maneuvers coordination were needed between different units too otherwise none would survive even an hour let alone win days weeks months engaged within such environment forces.

Urban Warfare Tactics

Urban warfare tactics have come a long way since the Battle of Stalingrad, when military strategists began to realize just how intricate and difficult it was fighting within cities. This engagement made clear the importance of logistics, intelligence and the integration of infantry, armor and artillery in city battles. Following this concept, modern armies have created specialized units and training courses designed specifically for urban combat requirements. Even now, the Stalingrad experience offers valuable insights into conducting war among densely populated regions.

Additionally, the Cold War strategic thinking of both NATO and Warsaw Pact forces was influenced by that same legacy. The need for large-scale combined operations, logistics support flexibility on distance fronts became some key principles embodied within future military plans after this time period. Throughout this era, each side prepared itself for conflicts potentially resembling those seen at Stalingrad in terms of magnitude or intensity . Hence, being able to maintain long lasting offensives became essential for military doctrine along with managing supply lines during extended campaigns being equally important.

Moreover, strategic teachings from Stalingrad affected infrastructure development and military technology growth. The battle experience created a demand for more advanced types of armored vehicles, engineering machinery or artillery pieces among other things used on earth works projects which had previously been unknown outside such contexts. Air power was recognized as critical due to the German attempts at airlifting supplies into encircled positions; thus both offensive anti–aircraft defences were significantly improved as well during this period . Hence; there is no doubt that combat support equipment became an essential part of modern day warfare through these innovations alone too Numerous other logistics related lessons have been learned since then;

Stalingrad's legacy is not just military strategy or technology, but life experience for many teenagers today. The battle was fought on such an epic scale that it became difficult for people to forget about what happened there and how they felt when hearing stories of the war later in life. Stalingrad turned into a city of heroes where everyone knew someone who had died fighting off the Nazis – either directly or through friends' relatives being killed during those times. After World War II ended national self-awareness among Soviet citizens changed forever with this one word: heroes – it represented shadows blended with light, horror seen alongside beauty.

Moreover, Stalingrad also represents the brutal truth about war. It was a total war which means many soldiers and civilians suffered greatly because there were no limits to the amount of violence used. Both military and political leaders have a duty to reduce harm during armed conflicts; this should be grounded on certain ethical norms that guide them through such processes. The battle of Stalingrad contributed significantly to the development of international humanitarian law, as well as military ethics thus demonstrating their importance even in modern day engagements.

In brief, the battlefields of Stalingrad witnessed great events with long-term effects. Having been a turning point in World War II it initiated series strategic operations conducted by the Soviet Union culminating into capturing Berlin. The principles learnt through fighting street by street, logistical challenges coupled with flexibility at different levels not only guided planning but also influenced various military doctrines over many years. More importantly however is that Stalingrad symbolizes indomitable spirit; this historic truth continues to be upheld nationally and globally where necessary.this essay writers give you professional help on any difficulty levels where required.

Key Figures of the Battle: Heroes and Leaders of Stalingrad

Several key figures directed the combat of Stalingrad, one of the most significant and bloody confrontations World War II. These persons, who ranged from high-ranking officers down to ordinary soldiers, played crucial roles that influenced the outcomes greatly through their leadership, bravery as well as tactical brilliance. Accounts of these people's lives during the Battle for Stalingrad are given in this article.

General Friedrich Paulus

In relation to the Battle of Stalingrad, Friedrich Paulus is probably one of its most famous figures. Born in 1890, he had an illustrious career in the military which saw him hold various staff appointments both during and after World War One. By the outbreak of World War Two, Paulus had been promoted through different ranks owing to his reputation for being highly organized while possessing good strategic planning skills.

Appointed as commander of the Sixth Army by Hitler himself in 1942, Paulus oversaw the assault on Stalingrad led by German forces. Although they achieved initial victories, his troops got caught up within ferocious street battles typical of this engagement thereby stalling any further progress. With the encirclement of Sovict army's counteroffensive around them becoming tighter and tighter each day; General found himself with no other option but to seek permission for breakout attempts which were however turned down repeatedly on orders from their superior officer who insisted that city must be held at all costs. Eventually promoted to rank of Field Marshal- historical title carrying expectation committing suicide rather than surrendering oneself into enemy hands- Paulus surrendered himself on 2nd February 1943 after realizing there was nothing more he could do to change fortunes of war. This act marked turning point in favor against Hitler's Nazi regime while also leading directly into his capture by Soviet forces. Following end of hostilities, he chose to reside within USSR before eventually moving over East Germany where up until death took place some years later during 1957; became outspoken critic against Nazism.

General Vasily Chuikov

Vasily Chuikov, born in 1900, served as a leading Soviet commander in the Battle of Stalingrad where he had to command the 62nd Army to defend the city. He displayed strong will to fight which is shown by never giving up in urban warfare plus bringing in new methods. It became a famous declaration when he said his troops would either keep Stalingrad or perish. His tactics involved close combat fighting as well as snipers to annoy and lower morale among German soldiers while protecting narrow paths over Volga River.

He encouraged soldiers through personal example and by being ready to join them at any time. Uniforms were abolished so that everyone could wear what they liked provided that it was warm enough. According to him "every street is a front – every house a blockhouse – the windows are loopholes". The condition under which this type of battle took place demanded great physical fitness together with mental alertness far beyond what is normally referred as necessary even during war time. A person who does not possess these qualities cannot but fail in an unequal struggle. Soviet troops were so deeply imbued with the spirit of national hatred towards the barbarous fascist invaders that they actually regarded themselves as mere tools for its satisfaction. In fact they were carrying out country's will rather than their own.

He had commanded soldiers personally too and it made them more confident about their victory. Those who showed initiative or did something outstanding were usually given some form of material encouragement. He used to say that the main value of this battle lay in the fact that it was being fought for by peoples fighting for their freedom against enslavement by Hitlerite Germany. Nobody can say that we are suffering from hunger since there is enough bread for everyone's need. On the contrary we have to fight against those who organize famine in order to subject us defenceless people to their will. The city defence had been entrusted entirely to NKVD border guards police and even militia units composed mainly of middle aged party workers without any military training whatsoever.

General Georgy Zhukov

Born on 1/9/1896 he joined Red Army in 1918. He got military education in 1920. In 1943 he became a Marshal of the Soviet Union. During the Battle of Stalingrad he was Deputy Commander-in-Chief and Commanded the 2nd Guards Army. Afterwards he played significant roles in Soviet military leadership till his death. He said that we cannot wait till enemy comes to us. It is needed to attack them when they are ready to move forward but still weak in terms of strength or numbers. Offensive operations should be carried out by those troops which feel better themselves than defensive ones.

Vasily Zaytsev

Vasily Zaytsev, born in 1915, was a Soviet sniper whose actions during the Battle of Stalingrad became legendary. Zaytsev's marksmanship and tactics were pivotal in the urban warfare environment of Stalingrad, where snipers played a crucial role. He is credited with killing 225 enemy soldiers during the battle, including several high-ranking German officers.

Zaytsev's exploits were widely publicised by Soviet propaganda, making him a national hero and a symbol of Soviet defiance. His memoirs and the stories of his sniper duels, particularly with an alleged top German sniper, became part of the mythos surrounding the battle. After Stalingrad, Zaytsev continued to serve in the Soviet military, eventually being promoted to the rank of Captain. His legacy endures as one of the most celebrated snipers in military history.

Field Marshal Erich von Manstein

Erich von Manstein, born in 1887, was one of Nazi Germany's most skilled strategists and played a significant role in the broader context of the Battle of Stalingrad. Although he did not command forces directly within the city, Manstein was tasked with leading the relief effort to break the encirclement of the Sixth Army. Operation Winter Storm, launched in December 1942, aimed to relieve Paulus's trapped forces but ultimately failed due to stiff Soviet resistance and logistical challenges.

Manstein's strategic acumen was evident in many other battles, and his failure to relieve Stalingrad was largely due to the overwhelming odds and the rigidity of Hitler's orders. After Stalingrad, Manstein continued to serve in high command positions and was known for his defensive strategies on the Eastern Front. His post-war memoirs provided detailed insights into the German military operations, although his role in the Nazi regime remains a point of contention.

Lieutenant General Vasily Gordov

In 1896, Vasily Gordov was born and became another one of the great Soviet generals who took part in the Battle of Stalingrad. Initially, he defended the city as a commander of the 21st army, and then he started counterattacking at its outskirts. He became one of the most important figures in Operation Uranus due to his ability to lead and cooperate with other Soviet commanders.

Even though he had been acknowledged for the success of USSR by gaining more ranks after this event, his last years were full of struggle because of inner political problems of the country; so much so that eventually Vasily got arrested during Stalin's purges and shot dead afterwards. Nevertheless, despite such tragic end lieutenant general's part played during this warfare serves as a perfect example for showing what he was capable of doing as a military leader.

Their actions and choices were the ones that defined what the Battle of Stalingrad would turn out to be; these along with many others who held key positions there. Such people were not only distinguished by their courage but also by strategic thinking which was so necessary during such a great conflict. It is through them we learn about individuals' place in history on top of everything else.

Bibliography

Comprehensive List of Sources and Further Reading on the Battle of Stalingrad

Books

1.   Beevor, Antony. *Stalingrad: The Fateful Siege: 1942-1943*. Penguin Books, 1998.

 - A comprehensive and detailed account of the Battle of Stalingrad, including personal stories and strategic analysis.

2.   Craig, William. *Enemy at the Gates: The Battle for Stalingrad*. Penguin Books, 1973.

 - A gripping narrative that combines first-hand accounts with historical analysis.

3.   Erickson, John. *The Road to Stalingrad: Stalin's War with Germany, Volume One*. Yale University Press, 1975.

 - Provides a detailed strategic and operational history of the Eastern Front leading up to Stalingrad.

4.   Glantz, David M., and Jonathan House. *Armageddon in Stalingrad: September-November 1942*. University Press of Kansas, 2009.

 - A meticulous study of the battle with a focus on the operational and tactical aspects.

5.   Hayward, Joel. *Stopped at Stalingrad: The Luftwaffe and Hitler's Defeat in the East 1942-1943*. University Press of Kansas, 1998.

- Examines the role of the Luftwaffe and its impact on the Battle of Stalingrad.

6.   Jones, Michael K. *Stalingrad: How the Red Army Triumphed*. Pen & Sword Military, 2007.

- Offers insights into the Soviet perspective and how they managed to achieve victory.

7.   Kershaw, Ian. *Hitler: 1936-1945 Nemesis*. W. W. Norton & Company, 2000.

- Provides context on Hitler's strategic decisions and their impact on the war, including Stalingrad.

8.   Roberts, Geoffrey. *Stalin's General: The Life of Georgy Zhukov*. Random House, 2012.

- A biography of General Zhukov, with significant coverage of his role in the Battle of Stalingrad.

9.   Snyder, Timothy. *Bloodlands: Europe Between Hitler and Stalin*. Basic Books, 2010.

- While not exclusively about Stalingrad, this book provides important context about the Eastern Front.

10.   Clark, Alan. *Barbarossa: The Russian-German Conflict 1941-1945*. Harper Perennial, 1965.

- An essential overview of the conflict between Germany and the Soviet Union, covering the broader context of the Battle of Stalingrad.

Articles and Papers

1.   Glantz, David M. "The Battle of Stalingrad." *The Journal of Slavic Military Studies*, Vol. 10, No. 1 (1997): 150-165.

   - A detailed scholarly article analyzing the strategic and operational dimensions of the battle.

2.   Mawdsley, Evan. "Crossing the Rubicon: Soviet Plans for Offensive War in 1940–1941." *International History Review*, Vol. 25, No. 4 (2003): 818-865.

   - Discusses Soviet strategic planning, providing context to the defensive operations at Stalingrad.

3.   Erickson, John. "The Road to Stalingrad: The Soviet-German War 1941-1943." *The Journal of Military History*, Vol. 37, No. 2 (1973): 205-223.

   - Examines the broader strategic movements leading up to Stalingrad.

Documentaries and Films

1.   "World War II in HD." History Channel, 2009.

   - A visually rich documentary series with episodes focusing on key battles, including Stalingrad.

2.   "The World at War." Thames Television, 1973-1974.

   - A comprehensive documentary series that includes detailed coverage of the Battle of Stalingrad.

3.   "Stalingrad." Directed by Joseph Vilsmaier, 1993.

   - A German film that portrays the harrowing experiences of soldiers during the battle.

4.   "Enemy at the Gates."** Directed by Jean-Jacques Annaud, 2001.

- A dramatized account focusing on the sniper duel within the battle, providing a cinematic perspective.

Online Resources

1.   United States Army Center of Military History. *Stalingrad to Berlin: The German Defeat in the East*.

- Official military history publications that provide detailed maps and strategic analysis. Available at: [CMH Online](https://history.army.mil/html/books/030/30-5-1/index.html)

2.   World War II Database (WW2DB).

- Offers detailed articles, maps, and photographs related to the Battle of Stalingrad. Available at: [WW2DB Stalingrad](https://ww2db.com/battle_spec.php?battle_id=10)

3.   Imperial War Museums (IWM).

- Provides access to a vast collection of photographs, documents, and oral histories related to the Battle of Stalingrad. Available at: [IWM Collections](https://www.iwm.org.uk/collections)

4.   BBC History.

- Features articles and interactive content on the Battle of Stalingrad and its significance. Available at: [BBC History Stalingrad] (https://www.bbc.co.uk/history/ worldwars/wwtwo/ battle_stalingrad _01.shtml)

Additional Reading

1.   Merridale, Catherine. *Ivan's War: Life and Death in the Red Army, 1939-1945*. Picador, 2006.

- Provides a social history of Soviet soldiers, offering insight into their experiences during battles like Stalingrad.

2.   Hart, Stephen. *Colossal Cracks: Montgomery's 21st Army Group in Northwest Europe, 1944-45*. Stackpole Books, 2007.

- While focused on a different front, it provides comparative insights into Allied operations that can contrast with Soviet tactics at Stalingrad.

3.   Overy, Richard. *Russia's War: A History of the Soviet Effort: 1941-1945*. Penguin Books, 1998.

- A broad history of the Soviet war effort, with significant coverage of the Battle of Stalingrad.

This comprehensive bibliography should provide a thorough foundation for understanding the Battle of Stalingrad, its historical significance, and its lasting legacy.